W9-BFN-067

How Serious Is Teen Drunk and Distracted Driving?

How Serious Is Teen Drunk and Distracted Driving?

Patricia D. Netzley

INCONTROVERSY

ReferencePoint
Press®

San Diego, CA

8/30/15 MTP

© 2014 ReferencePoint Press, Inc.
Printed in the United States

For more information, contact:
ReferencePoint Press, Inc.
PO Box 27779
San Diego, CA 92198
www.ReferencePointPress.com

LIBRARY OF CONGRESS CATALOGING-IN-PUBLICATION DATA

Netzley, Patricia D.
  How serious is teen drunk and distracted driving? / by Patricia D. Netzley.
    pages cm. -- (In controversy)
  Includes bibliographical references and index.
  Audience: Grade 9 to 12.
    ISBN 13: 978-1-60152-552-9 (hardback) -- ISBN 10: 1-60152-552-4 (hardback) 1. Teenage automobile drivers--Juvenile literature. 2. Drunk driving--Juvenile literature. 3. Distracted driving--Juvenile literature. I. Title.
  HE5620.J8N48   2014
  363.12'51--dc23
                                                                      2013009270

Contents

Foreword

In 2008, as the US economy and economies worldwide were falling into the worst recession since the Great Depression, most Americans had difficulty comprehending the complexity, magnitude, and scope of what was happening. As is often the case with a complex, controversial issue such as this historic global economic recession, looking at the problem as a whole can be overwhelming and often does not lead to understanding. One way to better comprehend such a large issue or event is to break it into smaller parts. The intricacies of global economic recession may be difficult to understand, but one can gain insight by instead beginning with an individual contributing factor, such as the real estate market. When examined through a narrower lens, complex issues become clearer and easier to evaluate.

This is the idea behind ReferencePoint Press's *In Controversy* series. The series examines the complex, controversial issues of the day by breaking them into smaller pieces. Rather than looking at the stem cell research debate as a whole, a title would examine an important aspect of the debate such as *Is Stem Cell Research Necessary?* or *Is Embryonic Stem Cell Research Ethical?* By studying the central issues of the debate individually, researchers gain a more solid and focused understanding of the topic as a whole.

Each book in the series provides a clear, insightful discussion of the issues, integrating facts and a variety of contrasting opinions for a solid, balanced perspective. Personal accounts and direct quotes from academic and professional experts, advocacy groups, politicians, and others enhance the narrative. Sidebars add depth to the discussion by expanding on important ideas and events. For quick reference, a list of key facts concludes every chapter. Source notes, an annotated organizations list, bibliography, and index provide student researchers with additional tools for papers and class discussion.

The *In Controversy* series also challenges students to think critically about issues, to improve their problem-solving skills, and to sharpen their ability to form educated opinions. As President Barack Obama stated in a March 2009 speech, success in the twenty-first century will not be measurable merely by students' ability to "fill in a bubble on a test but whether they possess 21st century skills like problem-solving and critical thinking and entrepreneurship and creativity." Those who possess these skills will have a strong foundation for whatever lies ahead.

No one can know for certain what sort of world awaits today's students. What we can assume, however, is that those who are inquisitive about a wide range of issues; open-minded to divergent views; aware of bias and opinion; and able to reason, reflect, and reconsider will be best prepared for the future. As the international development organization Oxfam notes, "Today's young people will grow up to be the citizens of the future: but what that future holds for them is uncertain. We can be quite confident, however, that they will be faced with decisions about a wide range of issues on which people have differing, contradictory views. If they are to develop as global citizens all young people should have the opportunity to engage with these controversial issues."

In Controversy helps today's students better prepare for tomorrow. An understanding of the complex issues that drive our world and the ability to think critically about them are essential components of contributing, competing, and succeeding in the twenty-first century.

Dangerous Driving

O n the morning of March 24, 2012, in Norwalk, Connecticut, sixteen-year-old Brianna McEwan decided to check her high school's webpage while driving her Toyota 4-Runner. As she used the keyboard of her handheld smartphone, she veered out of her lane and struck a jogger by the side of the road. Forty-four-year-old Kenneth Dorsey had been training for a marathon; he later died of his injuries. McEwan was arrested and subsequently found guilty of negligent homicide as well as unlawfully using a cell phone and driving in the wrong lane. In October 2012 she was given a suspended prison sentence as a youthful first-time offender.

> "You need to focus all your attention on what you're doing. It only takes a second to swerve a few feet."[1]
>
> — Norwalk, Connecticut police chief Harry Rilling.

Many people hoped that publicizing McEwan's case would make people think twice about engaging in the same kind of reckless behavior. As Norwalk police chief Harry Rilling says, "We tried to convey just how this incident illustrates how dangerous it is to be distracted while driving a 3,500-pound vehicle 35 to 40 mph. You need to focus all your attention on what you're doing. It only takes a second to swerve a few feet. Everybody should look at this and learn from it."[1]

A Serious Problem

According to the US Centers for Disease Control and Prevention (CDC) in 2013, each day more than fifteen people are killed and more than twelve hundred are injured in crashes that have been reported to involve a distracted driver. This estimate is based on studies by the National Highway Transportation Traffic Safety Administration (NHTSA) concluding that 25 percent of all police-reported traffic accidents are either directly or indirectly caused by driver inattention. However, this number is undoubtedly much higher, since drivers who have been in an accident are sometimes unwilling to admit that their inattention was the cause.

Experts on distracted driving have identified four types of distractions that cause accidents: visual, auditory, manual, and cognitive. A visual distraction is one that encourages the driver to look away from the road. An auditory distraction is any noise or sound that draws the driver's attention away from driving. A manual distraction results from the driver's decision to perform some manual task unrelated to driving, such as changing the radio station or fiddling with a cell phone. A cognitive (mental) distraction occurs when the driver is thinking about something other than driving. According to a 2011 study by the Governors Highway Safety Association (GHSA), when any two or more of these distractions occur at once, the distraction should be considered major and the risk of an accident significant.

Ignoring Laws

Many studies show that teens are the largest age group to be distracted while driving. The Automobile Association of America (AAA) reports that teens experience distracted driving almost a quarter of the time they are behind the wheel. The US Department of Transportation reports that 11 percent of all drivers under the age of twenty who had an accident that caused at least one fatality cited distracted driving as the reason for the accident. Moreover, according to *Consumer Reports* and the CDC, in 2012 teens and seniors had more driving accidents than the rest of the population in the United States.

Some states are trying to address the problem of distracted driving through laws. At the time of McEwan's accident, for example, Connecticut had a law specifically banning all novice drivers—defined as anyone under the age of eighteen or anyone with a learner's permit—from using any kind of cell phone (handheld or hands-free) while driving. The state also banned all drivers from

Distracted teen drivers represent a growing hazard on US roads and highways. Driving drunk or driving while texting are to blame for many accidents involving young drivers.

using a handheld cell phone while driving. However, McEwan ignored these laws, and many other people ignore them as well. In fact, at a February 2013 hearing to consider tougher distracted driving laws in Connecticut, Dorsey's girlfriend said, "I dare any one of you to drive for more than five minutes without seeing someone with a phone behind the wheel of a car."[2]

Likely Causes

Both the NHTSA and the AAA cite cell phone use as the number one cause of driver distraction. The number two cause is fiddling with other electronic devices, including the radio, a CD player, or an MP3 player. Other causes include eating, reaching for a moving object inside the vehicle, looking at an object or event outside the vehicle, reading, applying makeup, and turning around to talk to passengers.

Drunk driving is also a matter of concern, contributing to

the fact that motor vehicle accidents are the leading cause of death among teens. Of these deaths, roughly two thousand per year among teens aged sixteen to nineteen can be tied to alcohol use. According to studies in 2012, teen drunk driving rates have dropped more than 50 percent over the past two decades, even as cases of distracted driving have risen in many places. For example, in January 2013 officials in Saskatchewan, Canada, announced that in 2012—for the first time in the history of this province of more than a million people—more fatal car accidents were caused by distracted drivers than by drunk drivers. Teen-caused traffic deaths, alcohol-related or not, have also dropped 62 percent since 1975 in the United States.

Nonetheless, according to estimates by the CDC, high school teens drive after drinking roughly 2.4 million times a month. One in five of teen drivers involved in a fatal crash had consumed alcohol prior to the crash, and 81 percent of these had enough alcohol in their bloodstream to be considered legally drunk. Moreover, drivers aged sixteen to twenty are seventeen times more likely to die in a crash if they have a blood alcohol concentration of .08 or higher percent than if they have not been drinking. (Most US states consider .08 percent to be legally drunk.)

Tougher Laws

Experts say that more needs to be done to address the issue of teens driving while drunk or distracted. Some argue that these problems warrant new and/or tougher laws. In New Jersey, for example, where legislation was recently passed allowing full prosecution of and fines as high as $150,000 for cell phone users who cause a serious accident while driving, Assemblyman Albert Coutinho suggests that drivers need to face maximum penalties when their carelessness causes severe injury. He says, "Any driver willing to play Russian Roulette with other people's lives should face the stiffest penalties possible."[3]

But another New Jersey legislator, Senator Fred Madden, says that stiff penalties alone will not solve the problem. "We have done extensive work to strengthen our laws and penalties related to distracted driving, but it is clear we have to do more," he says.

"We must also find ways to prevent these activities and to educate drivers about the risks involved with texting and talking behind the wheel."[4]

Indeed, many experts believe that education is a key component in dealing with the problem of distracted driving. As the US government's website on distracted driving states, "The best way to end distracted driving is to educate all Americans about the danger it poses."[5]

However, a Bridgestone Americas, Inc. study reported in April 2012 found that more than 50 percent of teens aged fifteen to twenty-one knew the risks of distracted driving but did it anyway, believing that they were good enough drivers to engage in this behavior without having an accident. Angela Patterson, manager of Bridgestone's Teens Drive Smart Program, says, "People often believe they drive safely and responsibly, especially our newest drivers. However, we need to reinforce that it only takes one time—one sip of coffee, one change of the radio station, one glimpse at the cell phone—to cause or be involved in a crash that could have dire consequences."[6]

"The best way to end distracted driving is to educate all Americans about the danger it poses."[5]

— Official US Government website on distracted driving.

Facts

- According to a 2011 study by the Governors Highway Safety Association, most drivers are distracted 25 to 50 percent of the time while behind the wheel.

- Studies of accident reports indicate that between 15 and 30 percent of drivers have admitted to authorities that their accident was caused by distraction.

CHAPTER ONE

What Are the Origins of Concerns About Teen Driving Habits?

Adults have long been worried about teenagers driving while drunk and/or distracted. However, lawmakers did not begin to address these concerns in any meaningful way until the 1990s, when teenage accident rates were on the rise. Studies of this problem revealed that the number of accidents involving teen drivers was far more than would be expected given the number of teen drivers on the road. For example, when the Association for the Advancement of Automotive Medicine studied Utah crash statistics for 1992 to 1996, it found that although sixteen- and seventeen-year-olds made up only 4.9 percent of the driving population, they were involved in 15.4 percent (43,964) of the crashes.

Passengers

Experts concluded that the inexperience of teen drivers combined with impaired concentration—whether because of distractions or the use of alcohol—were the reasons this age group was so prone to having serious driving accidents. They also found that teenage passengers were a main cause of distractions for teen drivers. A study released in May 2012 by AAA found that a sixteen- or seventeen-year-old driver's risk of having a fatal car accident per mile driven increases 44 percent if the driver's passenger is also a teenager, and the risk doubles if two teen passengers are in the car and quadruples with three. A nationwide Texas Traffic Institute study of federal data on teen driving from 1999 to 2008 had similar results. Coauthor Bernie Fette says, "If you add one kid in a car [driven by a teenager], you double the risk of crash. With two kids, you triple it, and with three kids, it goes up by a factor of six."[7]

Fette's study also found that teenage drivers were more likely to get into serious accidents at night. In fact, it concluded that driving after dark is more likely to cause a fatal accident than driving drunk, speeding, or not wearing a seatbelt. Other studies looking at data from the same time period found that most of the serious crashes involving teenage drivers occurred between 5 p.m. and 9 p.m. and that fatal crashes most often took place between midnight and 6 a.m.

According to the Texas Traffic Institute study, nighttime driving remained extremely dangerous for teens even when they did not consume alcohol. However, other studies have suggested that reducing teens' access to alcohol reduced accidents as well. For example, a 1995 study by the NHTSA found that over the ten years since the passage of the 1985 National Minimum Drinking Age Act the number of fatal traffic accidents nationwide involving teens dropped by 13 percent. This law effectively raised the minimum legal drinking age nationwide to twenty-one by withholding federal transportation funds from any state that failed to make twenty-one its minimum age for purchasing and publicly possessing alcohol.

Florida

Such studies encouraged lawmakers to consider legislation that would severely limit the conditions under which teens could drive. The first state to take up such legislation was Florida, which in the

> "If you add one kid in a car [driven by a teenager], you double the risk of crash. With two kids, you triple it, and with three kids, it goes up by a factor of six."[7]
>
> — Bernie Fette, researcher for the Texas Traffic Institute.

1990s had a serious problem with teenage drunk driving. Florida was then a popular spring break destination for students from many parts of the country. Every March and April high school and college-age teenagers arrived in Florida on vacation, and this influx of young people created a party atmosphere that enticed not only the vacationers but teens living in Florida to drive drunk and/or to pay more attention to their teenage passengers than the road.

To combat this risky behavior, on July 1, 1996, Florida legislators enacted a law that restricted the hours during which teens with a Florida drivers license could drive. However, they decided to make this a graduated law—a law whereby restrictions are eased as drivers become older and more experienced behind the wheel. This law specifically targeted drivers younger than age eighteen.

For such drivers the law mandated that for the first three months, holders of a learner's license were not allowed to drive between 7 p.m. and 6 a.m. After the first three months they could drive until 10 p.m. The law also stated that learner's licenses had to be held for six months prior to eligibility for the intermediate license, and sixteen-year-old intermediate license holders were

Teens enjoy their spring break holiday in sunny Florida. The state's popularity as a spring break destination highlighted the growing problem of teen drunk driving and prompted legislators to act.

not permitted to drive without adult supervision between 11 p.m. and 6 a.m. For seventeen-year-olds, adult supervision was required from 1 a.m. to 6 a.m. In addition, as of January 1, 1997, all drivers younger than twenty-one were subject to a zero tolerance law mandating that any driver under age twenty-one caught driving with a blood alcohol level of 0.02 or higher automatically have his or her Florida driver's license suspended for six months..

More States Adopt Restrictions

Within months of the new law's enactment Florida began seeing a decrease in teen accidents, and in 1997, the first full year when all aspects of the graduated licensing law were in effect, a survey of Florida accident rates showed a 9 percent reduction in fatal and injury crashes involving fifteen- to seventeen-year-olds. In contrast, a study comparing Florida's crash data that same year with Alabama's, which had no such law, showed that Alabama had no reductions in fatal and injury crashes among teens.

Because of Florida's success, many people began calling on lawmakers throughout the United States to adopt similar laws. One of the most influential advocates of graduated driving laws (GDLs) targeting teen drivers was the American Academy of Pediatrics (AAP), which often advocates for laws and policies intended to improve teen health. In November 1996 the AAP published an article in the journal *Pediatrics* that called on governments to enact GDLs intended to lower the number of deaths and injuries among teen drivers.

As a result of such advocacy, many other states adopted GDLs in the late 1990s and early 2000s. Today forty-eight states and the District of Columbia restrict nighttime driving for teenagers, and forty-five states and the District of Columbia restrict the number and/or type of passengers a teenage driver can carry. In Louisiana, for example, no driver under the age of seventeen who has not had a certain amount of time behind the wheel can have more than one person under the age of twenty-one in the car between 6 p.m. and 5 a.m. In Connecticut, for the first six months of driving a teenager cannot carry any passengers except his or her parents or driving instructor, and for the second six months no passengers

Should the Drinking Age Be Lowered?

In the 1970s states that changed their laws to lower the minimum legal drinking age saw an increase in cases of drunk driving and soon raised the age again. Consequently no state is eager to return to a lower drinking age, especially since under the 1985 National Minimum Drinking Age Act it would mean losing federal funding. Nonetheless, some people have been calling for a lowering of the age based on two main arguments. First, they do not think it is fair that many states consider age eighteen the age of majority, which means that someone over eighteen is treated as an adult under the law, and yet eighteen- to twenty-year-olds cannot drink alcohol. Second, they say that prohibiting these young adults from drinking alcohol in public simply causes many of them to drink in private, which makes it harder to monitor alcohol intake and ensure that they do not get behind the wheel of a car drunk. However, opponents of raising the age say that whereas young people over the age of eighteen are generally mature enough to be treated as adults in other ways, alcohol is simply too difficult for this age group to handle responsibly.

except parents, a driving instructor, or immediate family. Such restrictions have served to reduce the possibility of being distracted by passengers while driving.

GDL Stages

The typical GDL has three stages: the learner stage, the intermediate stage, and the full-privileges stage. In the first stage teen drivers must always be supervised by an experienced driver while behind the wheel, and they must take a driving test administered by their state's Department of Motor Vehicles in order to move to the intermediate stage. Intermediate teen drivers are allowed to drive unsupervised under certain conditions that their state has deemed low risk, such as alone in the middle of the day. The final stage provides teen drivers with full driving privileges and a standard, unrestricted driver's license.

In addition, most states require teen drivers to be at the first stage, operating under the most restrictions, for six months before they can be considered an intermediate driver, providing they meet the minimum age requirement for being in the intermediate stage. Some states, however, require a twelve-month novice stage, and a few have no intermediate stage. There are also states that require a minimum number of supervised hours behind the wheel before a driver can move from the first stage to the intermediate stage.

For example, in Colorado—one of the more restrictive states when it comes to teen driving—a teen who has taken a course in driver's education can get a learner's permit at the age of fifteen, whereas a teen who has not taken a driver's education course must wait until age sixteen to get a learner's permit. The teen must then remain at the learner stage for at least twelve months, during which he or she must have a minimum of fifty supervised hours of driving and an additional ten hours of driving at night. To enter the intermediate stage, the driver must be age sixteen and can drive unsupervised any time except from midnight to 5 a.m. For the first six months of having an intermediate license, the teen driver cannot carry any passengers under the age of twenty-one except an immediate family member, and for the second six months no more than one passenger under the age of twenty-one who is not an immediate family member. Full driving privileges are not granted until age seventeen.

In Delaware, lawmakers have also included a seatbelt provision in their GDL. Any teenage driver who is caught not wearing a seatbelt, and/or who is carrying a teenage passenger not wearing a seatbelt, will lose his or her license for two months. In North Dakota, teen drivers are not allowed to drive any car not owned by a parent or legal guardian. In New Jersey, drivers under the age of twenty-one who do not have full-privilege licenses must display a decal on their vehicle that identifies them as new drivers.

A Successful Approach

As GDLs spread across the country, researchers began studying their effectiveness. One of the most notable of these studies was conducted by the Johns Hopkins Bloomberg School of Public Health in 2006. Using 1994–2004 data collected by the NHTSA and the US Census Bureau, that study evaluated the relationship between GDL programs and fatal crashes involving sixteen-year-old drivers. The study found that GDLs with certain characteristics were more effective than others.

The most successful GDLs restricted nighttime driving and carrying teen passengers, required teens to be at least fifteen-and-a-half years old to get a learner's permit, and required a minimum of thirty hours of driving under supervision. In addition they did not allow a teen to get an intermediate license less than six months after getting a learner's permit, did not allow anyone under the age of sixteen to get an intermediate license, and required teens to be at least seventeen for full licensure. States whose GDL had at least five of these characteristics had 18 percent fewer crashes involving sixteen-year-old drivers. States whose GDL had at least six of these characteristics had 21 percent fewer crashes involving sixteen-year-old drivers.

New Technology

But one of the main sources of distraction for teen drivers is not addressed by GDLs: cell phone use. In 1995, when the first GDL was being crafted, only about 13 percent of Americans owned cell phones, and the number of teens who used them was negligible. Therefore lawmakers did not consider these devices in crafting legislation meant to reduce driving distractions among teens. By 2011, however, 80 percent of Americans, including more than 75 percent of teens, had cell phones. Today many experts believe that nearly 95 percent of teens have them.

Initially, cell phones were a potential distraction only because they provided teens with a way to talk on the phone while driving. But the introduction of smartphones in the mid-2000s also allowed teens to send text messages (an activity known as texting)

The Car as a Personal Computer

Safety advocates have become concerned about a new trend among auto manufacturers to install Internet-connected computers on the front dashboard above the gearshift, where drivers can see and interact with them while driving. "This is irresponsible at best and pernicious at worst," says Nicholas A. Ashford, a professor of technology and policy at the Massachusetts Institute of Technology (MIT). "Unfortunately and sadly, it is a continuation of the pursuit of profit over safety—for both drivers and pedestrians." Car manufacturers counter that they are concerned with safety and will continue to make their devices safer to use. For example, Jim Buczkowski, who develops such technology for the Ford automotive company, says, "We are trying to make [the] driving experience one that is very engaging. We also want to make sure it is safer and safer. It is part of what our DNA will be going forward." Another automotive company, Audi, addresses the problem of driving distraction with a warning that is displayed on the screen whenever one of its Internet devices is turned on. It tells the driver, "Please only use the online services when traffic conditions allow you to do so safely."

Ashlee Vance and Matt Richtel, "Despite Risks, Internet Creeps onto Car Dashboards," *New York Times*, January 6, 2010. www.nytimes.com.

and surf the Internet while driving. In the latter half of the 2000s, smartphones also offered a GPS, or global positioning system, to help teens find their way from one place on a map to another, and looking at this information takes drivers' eyes off the road.

None of these features would be much of a problem if teens rarely used their phones. But teens who have cell phones typically use them heavily. According to the Pew Research Center, as of December 2011, 80 percent of young people aged fourteen to seventeen use cell phones on a regular basis. Other studies indicate that over 50 percent of teens send text messages every day, with more than half of them sending at least fifty text messages daily. An A.C. Nielsen study conducted in the second half of 2010 found that teens between the ages of thirteen and seventeen sent and received 3,339 text messages on their cell phones each month, whereas adults aged forty-five to fifty-four sent and received only 323 text messages a month.

By the end of 2010 over 40 percent of teenagers with cell phones were reporting that the reason they wanted a phone was so they could send text messages. In fact, Pew says, "Text messaging has become the primary way that teens reach their friends, surpassing face-to-face contact, email, instant messaging and voice calling as the go-to daily communication tool."[8] Perhaps for this reason, many teens ignore warnings that texting while driving is dangerous.

Inappropriate Times

Various studies have shown that teens have a greater tendency than adults to use their cell phones at inappropriate times. For example, less than one-fourth of all drivers admit to having sent text messages while behind the wheel, but nearly half of drivers under the age of eighteen say they engage in this behavior. Consequently, as the popularity of text messaging rose, so too did reports of cases where texting while driving led to a death.

Fernando Wilson and Jim Stimpson of the University of North Texas Health Science Center used accident reports from 2001 to 2007 supplied by the NHTSA to determine the effect of the increase in texting on accident rates in the United States. They write: "Our results suggested that recent and rapid increases in texting volumes have resulted in thousands of additional road fatalities in the United States. Since roughly 2001–2002, texting volumes have increased by several hundred percent. Since 2001 our model predicts that about 16,000 people have died since then that we attribute to the increase in texting volume in the United States."[9] Wilson and Stimpson also estimate

"Text messaging has become the primary way that teens reach their friends, surpassing face-to-face contact, email, instant messaging and voice calling as the go-to daily communication tool."[8]

— Pew Research Center.

Text messaging has become the primary means of communication for American teens. While many understand the dangers of driving while texting, they sometimes act without thinking—leading to car accidents and serious or even fatal injuries.

that the number of deaths caused by distracted driving increases 19 percent with every million new cell phone users, and in 2008 approximately one in six fatal vehicle collisions resulted from distracted driving.

A typical example of how texting causes a fatal accident is the case of seventeen-year-old Alexis Summers of Saxonburg, Pennsylvania. In November 2011, shortly after 10 p.m., she was killed when she smashed her car into a tree. The accident occurred because she veered off the road while texting, swerved to get back on the road, and lost control of her vehicle, which spun around before crashing.

Cell-Phone Laws

In an attempt to prevent more accidents like this, states passed laws restricting the use of cell phones while driving. The first such law, banning the use of handheld cell phones while driving, was enacted in New York in 2001, and gradually many other states banned handheld cell phones as well. After hands-free cell phones were invented and became yet another potential driving distraction, some states limited the use of these devices while driving, too.

As of the end of 2012 ten states plus Washington, DC; Guam; and the Virgin Islands prohibit talking on a handheld phone while driving, and thirty-three states and Washington, DC, prohibit new drivers from talking on a hands-free phone while driving. (In defining a "new" driver, some cite the driver's age while others say it depends on the number of months the person has been driving and/or whether the person has a regular license or a learner's permit.) No state currently bans both handheld and hands-free phone use for all drivers, although in nineteen states and Washington, DC, it is illegal for a school bus driver to use a cell phone while passengers are on the bus.

Also as of the end of 2012, thirty-nine states as well as Washington, DC, and Guam have made it illegal for any driver, regardless of age or number of years behind the wheel, to send or read text messages while driving. An additional six states prohibit new drivers from texting, and a few states fine drivers for texting if the texting led the driver to commit some other traffic violation.

In addition, in September 2012 Ohio banned texting while driving for both adults and teens. However, adults are still allowed to use handheld cell phones for purposes other than texting, whereas teens under eighteen cannot use a cell phone at all while driving except in a verifiable emergency. This law has proved difficult to enforce because police officers cannot tell just by looking whether someone is under the legal age to use a phone or whether a driver using the phone's keypad is texting or dialing. Nonetheless, it has received praise for banning teens from all other electronic communications devices in addition to phones, including MP3 players, GPS systems, on-board computers, and hands-free accessories.

Other Distractions

The first bans on using handheld electronic devices not involved with communication were enacted in the mid-2000s, often in response to concerns regarding the use of MP3 players while driving. However, drivers typically cannot be pulled over and cited simply for using devices like iPods, iPads, and video game players. Instead, a police officer has to notice the device after stopping the driver for some other infraction. Moreover, the penalty for breaking the law is only a small fine.

Music players, however, continue to be installed in cars, and there are no specific laws against using them while driving, even though concerns about distractions related to radios and CDs predate GDL laws. Stories of teens who got into accidents because they were fiddling with their car's music system are legion. Jarad Dewing, an essayist for the website Gawker.com, describes such an accident in writing about the death of his teenage brother: "It was December 4, 2003. My younger brother, Luke, had reached down to change a CD in his car stereo on his way to school that morning, when he crossed the double yellows and smacked into a pickup truck, headfirst. His legs were mangled beneath the crumpled dash."[10] Later, bone marrow from one of Luke's broken legs got into his bloodstream, traveled to his heart, and caused a fatal heart attack.

To address such situations, Connecticut enacted a distracted driving law that prohibits drivers from engaging in any activity unrelated to operating a motor vehicle in a way that makes the vehicle unsafe, and the District of Columbia specifically prohibits inattentive driving while operating a motor vehicle. Other states have laws against driving unsafely or negligently that can be used to prosecute distracted drivers. But it is highly unlikely that such laws will stop drivers from interacting with the features in their cars, talking to passengers, or eating or grooming themselves while driving. It is even difficult to convince some teens not to drink alcohol before driving. Therefore, despite laws designed to alter the behavior of teen drivers, concerns about factors that can compromise their driving abilities continue to grow.

"My younger brother, Luke, had reached down to change a CD in his car stereo on his way to school that morning, when he crossed the double yellows and smacked into a pickup truck, headfirst."[10]

— Jarad Dewing, essayist for Gawker.com, on the accident that killed his brother.

Facts

- According to a study by researchers at Monash University in Melbourne, Australia, drivers who use any kind of handheld device while behind the wheel are four times more likely to be injured in a serious crash.

- According to the National Safety Council (NSC), automobile crashes are among the top three causes of death in a person's lifetime.

- In 2009 *Webster's New World College Dictionary* named "distracted driving" its Word of the Year.

- A survey by *Seventeen* magazine and the Automobile Association of America (AAA) found that drivers aged eighteen and nineteen are more likely to engage in distracted driving than those aged sixteen and seventeen.

- More than 80 percent of nighttime crashes among sixteen- and seventeen-year-old drivers occur between the hours of 9 p.m. and midnight.

CHAPTER TWO

How Do Cell Phones Affect Teen Driving Habits?

I n June 2012 Massachusetts teenager Aaron Deveau became the first person in his state convicted under a law that made it a criminal offense to injure someone in a car crash while texting and driving. This charge stemmed from an accident on February 20, 2011, when Deveau was seventeen. That day, he sent and received 193 text messages. One of the last was sent at 2:34 p.m. while he was driving home from his job at a grocery store, and an answer to it was received at 2:35 p.m. A minute later Deveau swerved across the street's center line and crashed head-on into a Toyota Corolla driven by fifty-five-year-old Donald Bowley Jr. of New Hampshire.

Bowley suffered severe head trauma, and his passenger (his girlfriend, Luz Roman) suffered serious injuries as well. During Deveau's trial, police detective Thomas Howell—who had arrived on the scene shortly after the accident—said, "They looked like they were sunken into [the] vehicle—like they were almost folded into floor boards, almost like they were hugging each other because their arms were like entangled."[11] On March 10 Bowley died of his injuries, and Deveau was charged with killing him.

At his trial, prosecutors presented evidence that immediately after the crash he had continued to send and read text messages. Experts also testified that he subsequently deleted two of these messages, suggesting they might have included an admission that he had been texting while driving. Deveau testified that he had not been texting but had simply been distracted because he was thinking about all of the homework he had to do when he got home. He also said he could not remember ever texting while driving.

The jury did not believe him and, after he was found guilty, Bowley's sister, Donna Burleigh, said, "We hope this sends a message that it's not OK to text and drive."[12] The judge also said the verdict should be a message that people need to keep their eyes on the road at all times, and Deveau expressed remorse for not doing so. "I made a mistake," he said. "If I could take it back, I would take it back. I just want to apologize to the family."[13] (Bowley had three children.)

During sentencing, the judge gave Deveau maximum penalties: two-and-a-half years for Bowley's death and two years for operating a motor vehicle negligently while texting, with these sentences to run concurrently. He also ordered that Deveau's driver's license be suspended for fifteen years. However, because he was a young and first-time offender, the judge suspended all but one year of the sentence, which Deveau was ordered to spend in a county house of corrections. Some people expressed outrage at this, saying he should have been required to serve the maximum sentences.

"If I could take it back, I would take it back. I just want to apologize to the family."[13]

— Aaron Deveau, who killed a father of three while driving distracted.

Far Too Common

Deveau's case is notable for being among the first to link a teen's texting while driving to a homicide conviction. However, the circumstances surrounding the accident are unfortunately not uncommon. There are many reports of teens swerving their cars while texting and striking another car; sometimes they strike an object or a person instead, or flip their own car over.

However, sometimes texting while driving results in a slower response time or a lack of any response at all rather than an inability to control the car. For example, in October 2012 in Holton,

A Massachusetts prosecutor shows jurors a photograph of the 2011 crash involving teenager Aaron Deveau. Deveau was found guilty of killing another driver as a result of texting while driving.

Indiana, nineteen-year-old Jonathon Phillips was driving down a street at a speed of 38 miles an hour (61 kph) while texting when he felt his car go over a bump. He thought he had run over an animal, stopped his car and got out to check, and discovered he had hit and killed a fourteen-month-old child who had run into the road. After the accident officials released a statement saying, "Law enforcement cannot reiterate enough [that] driving a vehicle requires all of the driver's attention. Communication devices, radios, eating, reading material and applying makeup, to name a few, are all things officers observe on the roadways that distracts drivers and leads to tragedies such as this."[14]

Types of Distractions

However, studies have shown that when such crashes occur involving a teen driver, cell phone use—whether for texting or talking—was a far more likely cause of the distraction than reading, eating, listening to the radio, or applying makeup. According to the National Safety Council (NSC) in 2011, at least 23 percent of all traffic accidents—or about 1.3 million—involved cell phone use. Other studies have found that cell phone users between the ages of sixteen and nineteen are responsible for over 20 percent of fatal car crashes in the United States.

Cell phone use while driving causes so many accidents because it is a visual, manual, auditory, and cognitive distraction. That is, cell phones require users to look at them, fiddle with them, listen to them (in the case of a phone call as opposed to a text), and think about the conversation they provide. Theoretically, if two of those components are eliminated—specifically, the visual and manual distraction—then the risk that an accident will occur as a result of using a cell phone while driving will be greatly reduced. Hands-free phones provide this reduction in distractions because they allow users to place calls and carry on conversations without having to look at or handle the phone. Consequently states that have banned drivers from using handheld cell phones continue to allow the use of hands-free phones.

"Law enforcement cannot reiterate enough [that] driving a vehicle requires all of the driver's attention."[14]

— Official statement from Holton, Indiana, after a 2012 distracted driving accident that killed a toddler.

Cognitive Distractions

But some studies have shown that hands-free phones are no safer to use while driving than handheld ones. Experts say this is because both kinds of cell phones provide a cognitive distraction so significant it is dangerous all on its own. David L. Strayer is a professor of psychology at the University of Utah and one of the foremost experts on this subject. He explains that listening to the radio is a passive mental activity. Texting and talking, on the other hand, are active mental activities because they require the mind to come up with things to say. As a result, Strayer has found that "cell-phone conversations made drivers more likely to miss traffic signals and react more slowly to the signals that they did detect." Moreover, he states, "When a driver becomes involved in a cell-phone conversation, attention is withdrawn from the driving environment necessary for the safe operation of the vehicle."[15]

In a 2011 study Strayer and other researchers at the University of Utah found that the driving performance of 97.5 percent of college students fell 20 to 30 percent when they tried to talk on a cell phone while operating a driving simulator. In other studies conducted in regular vehicles, Strayer also found that even when road signs are pointed out to a driver talking on a hands-free cell phone, the driver quickly forgets having seen the signs. Strayer reports that his test subjects "were more than twice as likely to recognize roadway signs" when they were driving without the distraction of a cell phone and were "less likely to remember [the signs] if they were conversing on a cell phone."[16]

Other studies have shown that struggling to remember things associated with a phone conversation can diminish driving performance. For example, one study showed that it was hard for drivers to stay in their traffic lane while they were trying to recall a phone number. Another study found that memorizing and reciting a list—the way someone might do while trying to remember a grocery list dictated by a family member during a phone call—could diminish a driver's steering ability and braking time. The longer the list, the more trouble the driver had keeping the car in its lane.

Texting

Experts disagree, however, on whether talking on a cell phone while driving is more or less dangerous than texting while driving. A 2011 National Safety Council report found that cell phone conversations are involved in twelve times as many crashes as texting. However, according to the National Highway Traffic Safety Administration in 2011, texting while driving increases the risk of an accident by 2,300 percent. Other studies have found that texting while driving increases the probability of a crash by a factor of 20 times compared with 1.3 times for talking or listening to a cell

"Cell-phone conversations made drivers more likely to miss traffic signals and react more slowly to the signals that they did detect."[15]

— David Strayer of the University of Utah, on his research into distracted driving.

Cell Phone Use at Accident Scenes

People who oppose bans on cell phone use say that these devices can be critically important during an emergency. Indeed, this can be true. Cell phones allow drivers to call for help and/or to report a crime or an accident quickly. But there have also been cases where a driver passing by an accident scene while using a cell phone accidentally hit emergency personnel helping victims there. This was the case, for example, in 2010 in Illinois, where a state trooper conducting a traffic stop on an expressway was struck and seriously injured by a passing driver using a cell phone. Because of this incident, Illinois lawmakers began working on a bill banning the use of handheld cell phones while driving within 500 feet (152 m) of an emergency scene that has flashing lights. When the bill passed in May 2012, it included a ban on people sending picture and video messages while driving at any time or place. This addition was a response to concerns about people taking pictures at accident scenes to share on the Internet.

phone conversation and 2.8 times for dialing a cell phone.

But while experts disagree on the degree of risk involved with texting versus talking on a cell phone while driving, they agree that texting adversely affects a driver's reaction time to a degree that most find extremely serious. Researchers at the Texas Transportation Institute of Texas A&M University reached this conclusion in October 2011 after conducting a study that evaluated the reaction times of forty-two drivers aged sixteen to fifty-four who were navigating a vehicle on an 11-mile test track (17.6 km). These drivers were tested under two conditions. They drove the track once without distractions and a second time while sending and receiving text messages.

Each time, they were told to stop whenever a yellow light

flashed, and each time the researchers measured how quickly they responded. By the end of the test, researchers had discovered that texting added three to four seconds to the reaction time of drivers—if they managed to stop at all. While either reading or sending a text, a driver was eleven times more likely to drive right past the light, often not even noticing it. The head of the study, Christine Yager, concludes, "Essentially texting while driving doubles a driver's reaction time. That makes a driver less able to respond to sudden roadway dangers."[17]

Comparing Drivers

In another study of reaction time, *Car and Driver* magazine conducted a test using two drivers from different age categories: twenty-two-year-old Jordan Brown and thirty-seven-year-old Eddie Alterman. They tested each driver at two speeds, 35 miles per hour (56 kph) and 70 miles per hour (113 kph), and timed how quickly they braked upon seeing a red light. They also measured how far the cars traveled before coming to a complete stop and noted whether the drivers could stay in their lanes during the test. In addition, they compared the effects of driving while texting with the effects of driving while legally drunk but not using a cell phone.

This study showed that both men had as much or more trouble stopping within a safe distance while using a cell phone as they did while drunk. During one sequence, for example, at 35 miles per hour (56 kph) Brown's car traveled an additional 21 feet (6 m) past his normal stopping point while he was reading a text and an additional 16 feet (5 m) while writing a text, but his reaction time was nearly the same while drunk as when he was not drunk. At 70 miles per hour (113 kph) he went an additional 30 feet (9 m) while reading a text, an additional 31 feet (9.4 m) while writing a text, and an additional 15 feet (4.6 m) when drunk.

At 35 miles per hour (56 kph) Alterman went an additional 45 feet (14 m) while reading a message, an additional 41 feet (12.5m) while writing a text, and an additional 7 feet (2 m) while drunk. At 70 miles per hour (113 kph), whether reading or sending a text, Alterman's best effort after several tries still resulted in his car going more than 90 feet (27 m) past his normal stopping distance. In one of his tries, he traveled 319 feet (97 m) past where he should have stopped. Moreover, according to Michael Austin of *Car and Driver*, Alterman typically had his eyes off the road for an average of more than four seconds while texting, and he often drifted or veered out of his lane. In addition, both men sometimes failed to notice red lights.

Worse than Drunk Driving?

As a whole, the data suggest that when someone is reading a text or an e-mail on a phone while driving, it adds roughly 36 feet (11 m) to the car's stopping distance, and when the driver is sending a text it adds 70 feet (21 m). In contrast, a car being driven by someone who is legally drunk will take an average of just 4 feet (1 m) longer than normal to come to a stop. However, Austin warns that although the study makes drunk driving look relatively safe, this is definitely not the case. He says, "Don't take the intoxicated results to be acceptable just because they're an improvement over the

During an event intended to illustrate the difficulty of driving safely while texting, a Washington high school student tries to drive and text at the same time. Similar tests under controlled conditions have shown that texting drivers have dangerously delayed reaction times.

Texting Without Seatbelts

Far too often the consequences of a serious car crash have been made even worse by the fact that the people in the car were not wearing seatbelts. As an example of the magnitude of this problem, a recent survey conducted in Bethlehem, Pennyslvania, found that 27 percent of drivers and passengers, both teen and adult, failed to wear their seatbelts. Sometimes this failure is due to forgetfulness, but more often it is a case of the same kind of recklessness and inability to assess risk that leads teens to text while driving. Consequently it should be no surprise that many accidents related to texting also involve people who did not buckle their seatbelts. No studies have been done to determine just how often this is the case, but accident reports provide many examples of individuals thrown from a vehicle and seriously injured or killed. Those who survive such crashes typically say that it convinced them to always wear their seatbelts and no longer text in a car.

texting numbers. They only look better because the texting results are so horrendously bad. The buzzed Jordan had to be told *twice* which lane to drive in, and in the real world, that mistake could mean a head-on crash. And we . . . only measured response to a light—the reduction in motor skills and cognitive power associated with impaired [drunk] driving weren't really exposed here."[18]

Moreover, Austin believes that the drivers' results would have been much worse under real-world driving conditions. He explains, "We were using a straight road without any traffic, road signals, or pedestrians, and . . . Brown's method of holding the phone up above the dashboard and typing with one hand would make it difficult to do anything except hit the brakes. And if anything in the periphery required a response, well, both drivers would probably be screwed."[19]

To confirm these results, Phil LeBeau of CNBC news took

this test himself, and he believes that his results suggest texting and driving might actually be even more dangerous than drinking and driving. He reports, "When I took the test for . . . texting, I was just as slow to react [as the *Car and Driver* test subjects]. On average, it took me four times longer to hit the brake. Mike Austin at *Car and Driver* told me in blunt terms that I was 'way worse' than the average driver."[20]

Bad Drivers

Experts say, however, that despite such results, the public does not take the issue of cell phone use behind the wheel seriously enough. As LeBeau says, "The American public correctly views drinking and driving as wrong. But when it comes to texting and driving, we are not as outraged. Probably because many of us have done it and still do it . . . [even where it's banned]. Sadly, it will likely take more accidents and more deaths to change that attitude. There are countless stories of teens dying in accidents because the driver was texting while driving."[21]

However, some people believe that bad drivers, not cell phones, cause accidents, and that these bad drivers would still have accidents even if their phones were taken away. One such person is technology expert Timothy Geigner of Techdirt.com, who points to research that suggests "a driver capable of driving distracted on his cell phone will dutifully seek out other ways to be distracted if the phone is no longer an option."[22] Geigner points to a 2012 study by the Massachusetts Institute of Technology (MIT) in Cambridge, Massachusetts, to support this position.

The MIT study involved 108 drivers equally divided by age among those in their twenties, forties, and sixties. Test subjects began the study by answering a driver behavior questionnaire (DBQ) about their driving habits, including how fast they typically drove and how often they used a cell phone while driving. They were also asked whether and under what conditions they had received warnings or tickets from police for bad driving. They were then divided into two groups, those who fre-

> "A driver capable of driving distracted on his cell phone will dutifully seek out other ways to be distracted if the phone is no longer an option."[22]
>
> — Timothy Geigner of Techdirt.com.

quently used cell phones while driving and those who infrequently used cell phones while driving. Each person in both groups was then given a Volvo SUV to drive for forty minutes on an interstate highway near Boston. During the drive, they were monitored by a variety of devices in order to determine how well they drove and how agitated they became while driving. These devices included video cameras, heartbeat sensors, and an eye tracker, which is a head-mounted tracking device that records where a person's eyes are focused. However, the drivers had no cell phones with them.

In evaluating the data, researchers discovered that frequent and infrequent users differed dramatically in how they drove. They stated:

> Individuals who reported frequently using cell phones while driving were found to drive faster, change lanes more frequently, spend more time in the left lane, and engage in more instances of hard braking and high acceleration events. They also scored higher in self-reported driving violations on the DBQ and reported more positive attitudes toward speeding and passing than drivers who did not report using a cell phone regularly while driving. These results indicate that a greater reported frequency of cell phone use while driving is associated with a broader pattern of behaviors that are likely to increase the overall risk of crash involvement.[23]

In reporting on the study, one of its leaders, Bryan Reimer, was careful to say that its findings did not indicate that cell phone use while driving was not dangerous. "There is no question in anyone's mind that talking on a cell phone increases risk," he stressed. However, he added that drivers who would be at greater risk for getting into an accident while using a cell phone "may be the drivers who are getting in accidents anyway."[24]

"Crappy Drivers Are Crappy Drivers"

If this is the case, Timothy Geigner suggests, then it is pointless to take away drivers' cell phones. In commenting on the MIT study's conclusions he says:

In other words, crappy drivers are crappy drivers. If they aren't chattering away on their phones, they'll be singing Carly Rae Jepson with their eyes closed, or putting on their deodorant, or reaching into the backseat for that bag of Cheetohs they left there last weekend. But do we ban cheese snacks in cars? Do we outlaw Old Spice-ing while driving? Should pop music be banned in the car (resist . . . temptation . . . to say . . . yes . . .)? Of course not, particularly when these studies continue to show that distractible drivers will find another way to run us all over.[25]

But others counter that if cell phones were not a big part of the problem, then accident rates would not go down wherever cell phones are banned. One such place is California, where a 2012 study by the University of California at Berkeley found the state's ban on drivers using handheld cell phones resulted in a 22 percent reduction in traffic deaths overall and a 47 percent reduction in deaths that could directly be blamed on drivers using cell phones. Critics of the ban say these deaths could be attributed to other factors, or it might simply be that because of the ban more drivers are hiding their cell phone use from authorities investigating accidents. But supporters argue that the problem of distracted driving will always be lessened by the removal of a major form of distraction.

Facts

- According to the Virginia Tech Transportation Institute, sending or reading a text takes a driver's eyes off the road for 4.6 seconds, which at 55 miles per hour (88 kph) is the equivalent of driving the length of a football field blindfolded.

- Accident reports indicate that over 10 percent of all drivers under the age of twenty involved in fatal crashes were distracted at the time of the accident.

- Pew Research reports that 40 percent of American teens have confessed to being in a car when the driver used a cell phone in an unsafe manner.

- The National Safety Council reports that whereas in 1995 only 13 percent of the US population had cell phone subscriptions, by 2009 the number had increased to 91 percent.

- In 2011 California law enforcement officers issued more than 460,000 tickets for driving while using a handheld cell phone.

CHAPTER THREE

Are Teen Drivers More Susceptible to Distractions?

I n August 2012 fifty-two-year-old David Alan Shelley of Warwick, Pennsylvania, was supervising his sixteen-year-old daughter as she drove the family's Honda Odyssey minivan to sports tryouts at her high school at around 8:25 a.m. on a Saturday morning. The girl had a learner's permit and was driving well when she became distracted by a check engine light on the dashboard. She then veered off the right side of the road but was able to get the minivan back onto the road. However, her tires went over the dots on the center line of the road, which caused a noise that startled her, and she then veered off to the right again. This time the passenger side of the minivan struck a tree. Her father was fatally injured and died at the hospital the following evening. She was unhurt.

Overconfidence

Many new drivers have trouble keeping their eyes on the road, and as the Virginia Tech Transportation Institute (VTTI) reports, whether a driver can remain focused on the road is the key factor in determining the likelihood that the driver will have an accident. Perhaps it is no surprise, then, that studies indicate that 16 percent of all crashes related to distracted driving are caused by the youngest and most inexperienced drivers. These drivers also have more of a tendency to be overconfident about their driving ability. In Australia, for example, surveys conducted by the Royal Automobile Club (RAC) have shown that nearly 80 percent of young people believe they are better drivers than others their age. Consequently one of the heads of the RAC, Matt Brown, says, "Young people aren't making the connection that their own inexperience puts them at greater danger of having a serious, perhaps fatal, road accident."[26]

"Young people aren't making the connection that their own inexperience puts them at greater danger of having a serious, perhaps fatal, road accident."[26]

— Matt Brown of the Royal Automobile Club.

Research shows that this overconfidence typically occurs after six to twelve months of driving. Seattle, Washington, insurance company PEMCO reports that among its policyholders, the accident rate of sixteen-year-olds is not that much higher than that of adults, but the rate for seventeen-year-olds is three times the adult rate. The company says this is because after a year these drivers have "driven from home to school to home repeatedly, and they begin to think they've mastered driving. They haven't. They've only mastered their 'regular' trips, where they know every curve, intersection, and lane change. That doesn't mean they're good at judging new situations for the first time, especially if it's under difficult conditions (other teens in the car, dark outside, bad weather, etc.). They're still 'intermediate' drivers playing in an 'advanced' tournament, and they have a long way to go before they can perform at that level."[27]

PEMCO also notes that the overconfidence of these drivers often leads them to think they can drive any car just as well, when in fact different cars drive differently. Some vehicles take longer to brake, for example, or do not provide good visibility when looking out side windows. The placement of features inside the car can also be different. Consequently a driver needs to concentrate more when driving an unfamiliar car and pull over if there is any confusion about the car's features. Adult drivers are far more likely to do these things than teenage drivers.

Eating While Driving

Overconfidence can also prevent teens from understanding that seemingly minor activities can be major distractions. For example, a majority of teens think that changing the station on a radio is a relatively inconsequential action. According to a survey by *Seventeen* magazine and AAA, 73 percent of teens admit to having adjusted a CD or radio while driving. However, according to the AAA, changing CDs or radio stations is the second most common cause of accidents. (Using a cell phone is the leading cause.)

Similarly, a 2012 survey by the Insurance Institute for Highway Safety found that teens do not consider reaching for or consuming food or a beverage while driving a distraction. Yet according to AAA, eating in the car is the third most common cause of accidents. The NHTSA reports that drivers who eat and drink while driving increase their odds of having an accident by 80 percent.

Texting is not the only distraction for teen drivers. Eating and drinking while driving vastly increase the odds of having a car accident. Looking away from the road even for a few moments to take care of a coffee spill can be disastrous.

Spills

Experts believe there are three reasons for this increase. The first is that reaching for food or a beverage while driving typically requires drivers to take their eyes off the road long enough to grab the item and perhaps also unwrap it. In fact, studies by the VTTI indicate that reaching for anything while driving increases the risk of an accident by 1.4 times.

The second reason that eating while driving increases accident risk is because of the possibility of spillage. In many cases a driver has gotten into an accident while reacting to a spilled drink, especially hot coffee in the lap. For example, in October 2011 eighteen-year-old Catherine Bezanson of Bel Air, Maryland, crashed through a fence and went over a small cliff after spilling coffee in her Volvo. She says, "I bought coffee for my family and I was trying to come out of the parking lot, but the coffee spilled and I thought I put my foot on the decelerator, but I hit the wrong pedal and as I reached over to fix the coffee spill, the car went with me." She was not hurt, but she did learn something: "If coffee spills in your car, don't think about the coffee," she said. "Think about getting to your destination, turning your car off first, then fixing the problem, because it's definitely not worth it."[28]

"If coffee spills in your car, don't think about the coffee."[28]

— Catherine Bezanson of Bel Air, Maryland, after her coffee spill caused her to crash her car.

Reaction Time

The third reason that eating while driving increases accident risk has to do with reaction time. Studies have shown that even when drivers keep their eyes on the road while eating, they still respond more slowly than when they are not eating. A study by researchers at the University of Leeds in England found that drivers who ate a snack while driving reacted 44 percent slower than usual when required to brake. Drivers sipping a drink reacted 22 percent more slowly. In addition, whether eating or drinking, the drivers in the study were 18 percent more likely to have trouble staying in their driving lane.

The Leeds researchers compared their results with previous UK studies showing that drivers sending text messages had a 37.4

The Most Dangerous Foods

The NHTSA has developed a list of the foods and beverages that are the most dangerous to consume while driving. At the top of the list is coffee, because it is often extremely hot and can be spilled in the lap or sloshed out of a cup holder when the car hits a bump or swerves. In fact, studies show that because of these problems, crashes caused by beverage spills have increased with the popularity of Starbucks. Second on the list is hot soup, for the same reasons as coffee. The rest of the items save one are foods that tend to fall apart and/or drip while being eaten and can make a driver's hands and steering wheel messy: tacos, foods smothered in chili (such as chili dogs), hamburgers, foods slathered with barbecue sauce, greasy fried chicken, filled or powdered donuts, and warm chocolate bars. Also on the list (at number nine) are soft drinks, whether in an open cup or in a closed bottle; the former can be spilled, while the latter can fall on the floor and roll away from the driver—perhaps even under the brake pedal.

percent slower reaction time, driving drunk a 12.5 percent slower reaction time, and having a hands-free cellphone conversation a 26.5 percent slower reaction time. This led them to conclude that eating while driving is more dangerous than using a cell phone while driving—a worrisome conclusion considering the survey by *Seventeen* magazine and AAA found that 61 percent of US teens eat while driving.

Getting Lost

An increasing number of teens also use GPS devices while driving to avoid getting lost. In fact, nearly 50 percent of all drivers report having used these devices while behind the wheel, and many states acknowledge the importance of navigational devices by specifically exempting them from bans on electronic devices. This is because some experts believe that the confusion and frustration that comes with getting lost can increase the risk of an accident.

Others, however, share the view of Tim Hollister, who writes a blog for parents of teen drivers. He says, "In my opinion, we should not even be debating whether teen drivers should use a GPS. . . . [J]ust because a GPS is legal doesn't mean that it does not increase the already considerable danger of teen driving." Because GPS devices typically have screens and a keyboard much like cell phones, Hollister considers them serious distractions, and he questions whether teens really need them. He says that "one of the most important steps that should precede every time a teen driver gets behind the wheel [is] planning the intended route."[29]

However, studies indicate that teens behave in ways that make them more likely to get lost during a drive even after preplanning. For example, in surveys conducted in 2010 by the marketing firm Galaxy Research in Australia, 20 percent of teens reported that they would duck down a side street in order to avoid getting stuck in traffic even if it meant they might lose their way. (In contrast, only 6 percent of drivers over the age of fifty reported being willing to do this.) Teen drivers were also three times more likely to make impulsive decisions regarding their route in comparison with other age groups, and one-third of them reported having a poor sense of direction. Perhaps it is not surprising, then, that many studies have shown that drivers under age eighteen are the most likely to get lost while driving.

Overall, according to a 2011 Harris poll, 41 percent of drivers admit to having set or changed the address on a GPS device while driving, an activity that takes their eyes from the road for a considerable amount of time. But the alternative to using a GPS also does this: reading a map, a practice that 36 percent of all drivers admit to having done. There are no statistics on just how dangerous either of these activities is, however. As Humphrey Taylor, chairman of the Harris Poll, explains:

"Just because a GPS is legal doesn't mean that it does not increase the already considerable danger of teen driving."[29]

— Tim Hollister, parenting blogger.

The number of drivers who engage in potentially dangerous, in some cases extremely dangerous, behaviors while
driving is terrifyingly high, particularly when you remember that every 1 percent of drivers polled represents
more than one-and-three-quarters of a million people. . . .
While we have some information on how dangerous some
of these behaviors are (driving after drinking, talking on
cellphones, falling asleep, texting) we can only speculate as
to the numbers of accidents and deaths that are caused by
the many millions of people who drive while setting their
GPS, eating or drinking, surfing the Internet, watching
videos, combing their hair, reading or applying makeup.[30]

Impulsivity and Risk-Taking

Surveys consistently show that young people are more willing than
older people to use not just cell phones but any kind of handheld
device while driving. This does not mean they have a greater need
to use these devices than do older people. Instead it has to do
with their tendency to reach for things on impulse without thinking about the consequences. According to the University of North
Carolina Highway Safety Research Center:

By virtue of their continuing cognitive, social, emotion
and biological development, young drivers—especially
16-year-olds—tend to engage in impulsive behaviors.
When driving, these can be dangerous. Lack of driving
experience contributes to young drivers' inability to consistently recognize the conditions that are risky when driving. The presence of other teen occupants in the vehicle
with a young driver often compounds their tendency to
engage in impulsive behavior.[31]

As the research center's studies have noted, teens' impulsiv-
ity is often coupled with a greater tendency to take risks. This in
turn makes them more likely to put themselves in situations that
increase the likelihood that distractions will occur. For example,
teens are far more likely to drive faster than is safe, which is why

GPS devices are useful tools for drivers of all ages, but fiddling with them while on the road is another risky distraction. Destination information should be programmed into a GPS at the start of a trip or after pulling off the road and parking.

accident reports indicate that one-third of teen fatalities involve speeding. According to a University of North Carolina Highway Safety Research Center study of drivers aged sixteen to eighteen, teens were also likely to turn around while driving in order to talk to passengers, although males did this twice as often as females. Moreover, when near collisions and other serious driving events occurred during the study, horseplay and loud conversations were usually factors in cases where teen drivers had teen passengers.

Minimizing Risk

The study also found that in cases where teen drivers were alone in the car, nearly half of the serious driving events were associated with taking eyes off the road. Most drivers looked away for less than two seconds, but some looked away for at least four seconds, and females looked away more often than males. But the teens did not see this as risky behavior.

Other researchers have found that teens typically have less of an ability to assess risk than adults. This means that they minimize the chances that their actions will lead to dire consequences. For example, in the survey by *Seventeen* magazine and AAA, 35 percent of teens told researchers that they engaged in distracted driving because they did not think they would get hurt, and 41 percent said they engaged in this behavior because it only took a second. Some teens' reasons were more about feelings; 21 percent said they used cell phones because they had to remain connected to other people all the time, and 22 percent said they needed to use devices while driving because otherwise they were bored.

Multitasking

Many teens try to do several things at once and believe they are good at multitasking. However, the NSC says there is no such thing as multitasking. In a report on the problem of cell phone use while driving, the organization states: "Multitasking is a myth. Human brains do not perform two tasks at the same time. Instead, the brain handles tasks sequentially, switching between one task and another. Brains can juggle tasks very rapidly, which leads us to erroneously believe we are doing two tasks at the same time. In reality, the brain is switching attention between tasks—performing only one task at a time." The NSC adds that along with switching attention between tasks, "the brain engages in a constant process to deal with the information it receives."[32] Specifically, it selects the information it wants to attend to, processes that information, encodes that information—whereby memories are created—and stores the information.

> "Multitasking is a myth. Human brains do not perform two tasks at the same time."[32]
>
> — National Safety Council.

When there is too much information to deal with, the brain has to ignore some of it, and this can cause problems for drivers because some of this weeding out of information is done subconsciously. The NSC explains: "The brain is overloaded by all the information coming in. To handle this overload, the driver's brain will not encode and store all of the information. . . . The brain doesn't process critical information and alert the driver to potentially hazardous situations. This is why people miss critical warnings of navigation and safety hazards when engaged in cell phone conversations while driving."[33]

In studying this problem, psychology professor Ira Hyman of Western Washington University in Bellingham sought to determine just how distracted a cell phone user can become. To this end, Hyman asked one of his students to put on a clown costume and ride a unicycle on campus. He discovered that only 25 percent of people who walked past the clown while talking on a cell phone noticed him.

Inattention Blindness

Hyman also discovered that more than double this number noticed the clown if they were having a conversation with a person walking beside them rather than with someone on a phone. He therefore concluded that the cell phone, not the conversation, was what caused them to fail to see something that should have been obvious—a phenomenon called inattention blindness. Scientists have theorized that this "blindness" occurs because people create pictures in their minds while talking on the phone, and the brain has difficulty processing both imagined and real images at the same time.

For teens this problem is compounded by driving inexperience. David L. Strayer has found that teens generally have far more trouble than adult drivers trying to drive and do anything else at the same time because "they're just learning how to drive, so some of the things that a more experienced driver might have automated or become habitual are still quite effortful for a teen driver."[34]

Other researchers believe that the problem is more about the conscious brain and a lack of focus. For example, one of the researchers in the Galaxy Research study, Mark McCrindle, told reporter Richard Read that the upbringing of today's teens has made them overstimulated and less able to concentrate. According to Read, McCrindle believes that because teens "grew up with cable TV and the internet, and [are] rabid consumers of social media . . . they're less able to filter out irrelevant data and focus on what's important—for example, getting through a clogged intersection."[35]

The Parent-Teen Relationship

In November 2012 Toyota Motor Sales, U.S.A. and researchers from the University of Michigan Transportation Research Institute released the results of a major study involving not only teen drivers aged sixteen to eighteen but their parents as well. The study found a strong correlation between how both groups drive and determined that parents' driving behavior can influence teens' driving behavior. However, the study also showed that what teens think their parents do while driving is more important than what parents actually do. For example, if a teen thinks his or her parent eats while driving, that teen is two times more likely to eat while driving. In addition, teens' perceptions regarding their parents' behaviors are not always accurate. For example, 32 percent of teens think their parents use an electronic device for music while driving, when in fact only 10 percent do, and 71 percent of teens believe their parents read or write down directions while driving when only 55 percent do. Researchers have therefore concluded that parents need to talk more about their driving behavior in addition to modeling good behavior.

Behavioral Issues

Still others say that teens are more likely to drive distracted because of a carefree desire to have fun. This aspect of the problem is borne out by research that shows that teens are more likely to get into an accident during the summer months, when more time is devoted to play. According to the NHTSA, the period between Memorial Day and Labor Day is the most deadly for US drivers aged fifteen to twenty, and evening crashes are more common among teens in the summer as well. Justin McNaull of the Automobile Association of America explains why: "For many kids, every day in the summer is a weekend day. There's less parental supervision in the daytime because Mom and Dad are at work. In the evening, curfews get slid back, and they spend more time on purposeless trips, which are more dangerous. Driving with your buddies to find a party at 10 p.m. is very different from driving to school at 7 a.m. on a weekday. There's a very different environment both outside and inside the vehicle."[36]

McNaull reports that inexperience is also a factor in summer accidents because a more experienced driver is better equipped to handle distractions from other people in the car. He says that while driving with friends, teens "miscalculate while trying to make a left turn, or they rear-end somebody," and "when young drivers and their friends are driving to fast-food places or looking for a party, that's when you see more of the crashes related to immaturity, wanton risk-taking,"[37] especially at night.

However, the presence of passengers in the car does have one benefit to inexperienced drivers: It makes it less likely that a teen driver will use a cell phone while behind the wheel. *Seventeen* magazine and AAA report that only 20 percent of teens will text while driving if there are other teenagers in the car, whereas 35 percent of teens driving alone in their own car will engage in this activity. Teens also, understandably, drive more cautiously with adults in the car. However, studies show that even with parents along, novice drivers are sixteen times more likely than experienced drivers to glance at something inside the car, and the National Transportation Safety Board (NTSB) says that taking one's eyes off the road for just two seconds separates safe driving from dangerous driving.

Facts

- According to a study by Carnegie Mellon University in Pittsburgh, Pennsylvania, the brain of someone who is using a cell phone while driving devotes 37 percent less activity to driving.

- According to the NHTSA, whereas only 19 percent of drivers aged forty-five to sixty-five send text messages while driving, 44 percent of those under the age of twenty do.

- The NHTSA reports that only 6 to 9 percent of drivers under the age of twenty-five are willing to pull the car over before sending a text message.

- In surveys, when asked whether they were involved in a crash or near-crash within the past year, nearly 18 percent of males under age twenty said yes, compared with roughly 6 percent of females. In contrast, less than 4 percent of men and women aged sixty-five and older said yes.

- The Pew Research Center reports that the highest incidence of distracted driving occurs in the under-twenty age group.

- Studies show that drivers under twenty-five are two to three times more likely to text or e-mail than are older drivers.

CHAPTER FOUR

How Can Teens Be Convinced Not to Drink and Drive?

On December 29, 2011, just after 3 a.m. in Silver Spring, Maryland, three young people returning home from a nightclub together were in a car crash after the driver lost control of her Nissan Murano on a curve while going 91 miles per hour (146 kph) in a 40-miles-per-hour zone (64 kph). The car left the roadway, flew into the air over a fence, and landed in a yard before crashing into a wall and hitting a tree with such force that the impact wrapped the wreckage around the trunk. Pieces of debris were also flung up into the tree's branches and onto nearby utility wires. Both the driver, twenty-two-year-old Jenice Richards, and her backseat passenger, nineteen-year-old Tamara Nicole Johnson, were killed in the crash, which lasted only six seconds. The front seat passenger, eighteen-year-old Desaleen Rayna James, survived with serious injuries, including a broken hip.

The girls' friends were devastated by what had occurred. One of them, Queen Walker, who had seen them at dinner before they left for the club, said, "It hurt because I didn't get to say goodbye to [Johnson]."[38] This grief was compounded by the fact that the crash was caused by reckless behavior: Not only was Richards speeding but she was driving drunk. Police later determined that at the time of the crash, she had an amount of alcohol in her bloodstream that was twice the legal limit for intoxication.

A Shocking Videotape

Fatal crashes caused by drunk driving are not rare. According to AAA, drunk driving is the fifth most common cause of accidents, followed by drug use. Of the sixteen- to seventeen-year-olds killed in crashes, one in six were so drunk that they were beyond the legal limit for intoxication. Richards's crash was unique in that James, her surviving passenger, had made a video recording of events before, during, and after the crash that took her friends' lives. In May 2012 she began sharing this recording with news media as a way to show others the horrific results of choosing to drive drunk.

The beginning of the video shows the girls at the nightclub, where James is being served alsochol even though she is under-age. This had to do with the way in which the club determined whether each patron was old enough to drink. They had to show identification at the club's entrance, and the hand of anyone underage was marked with an "X" to show they were not to be served alcoholic beverages while there. But James later told a reporter, "It was very easy [to get around this]. I just had to pay the guy at the door ten dollars not to put an X on my hand. That was it."[39]

When the teens left the club, Richards and James were fully aware that they were drunk. In fact, right before the crash they were joking about this. On the tape it is difficult to make out which girl said what, but at one point someone shouts, "We're driving drunk!" and just moments before the crash one of them says, "If we die tonight, we know where we're going,"[40] meaning that they would be going to hell for behaving so badly. Johnson, the teen who had not been drinking, urges the driver to slow down. Then the accident occurs, accompanied by nightmarish sounds, and the video recorder continues to run for another twenty-one minutes as rescue workers arrive on the scene and deal with the aftermath.

"You never think that something like this is going to happen to you. It's one in a million, like, and then boom. It hits you."[41]

— Desaleen James, survivor of a drunk driving accident.

Facing Criticism

In the months that followed, James had a hard time recovering from the physical and emotional trauma of the accident. Still, she set aside her mental anguish in order to go before the public to speak of the dangers of drunk driving. She says, "You never think that something like this is going to happen to you. It's one in a million, like, and then boom. It hits you. And there you are, that one in a million. . . . If you want to put yourself in that position . . . [y]ou're putting yourself out there to die."[41]

James's warnings did not bring the result she hoped for. After her story aired, she received hate mail from teens who called her a "snitch" for revealing how easy it was for teens to get alcohol in a Maryland nightclub. These teens were afraid that the publicity James attracted would result in club owners making it more difficult for them to continue getting alcohol illegally, too.

Experts estimate that 40 percent of alcohol-related fatal traffic crashes in the United States involve teen drivers. Statistics like these do not seem to sway teens who openly admit to drinking and driving and see nothing wrong with it.

Binge Drinking

Many teens see nothing wrong with consuming alcohol even though it is illegal for them to do so. In fact, in many cases a teen driver involved in a drunk driving accident will have exhibited previous tendencies to drink to excess. In a survey reported by the CDC, 85 percent of high school students who admitted to drinking and driving within the previous month also admitted that they engage in binge drinking.

In other studies, teens have admitted to being more likely to drink excessively when partying with other teens. Research has shown that during spring break, a common time for partying, more than half of teenage boys and more than 40 percent of teenage girls reported drinking until they became severely intoxicated. And this behavior is not limited to older teens; statistics indicate that one out of every ten teens between the ages of twelve and thirteen drink alcohol at least once a month.

A significant number of teens also see nothing wrong with getting behind the wheel while drunk. Of the roughly 12 percent of all fatal traffic crashes in the United States that are alcohol-related, experts estimate that 40 percent involve teen drivers. In some of these cases the drinking did not just occur before driving but while driving. However, the CDC reports that the number of teens who think it is okay to drink and drive varies widely across the United States. More than twice as many teens in Texas, for example, openly admit to drinking and driving than teens in Colorado (roughly 15 percent versus approximately 6 percent).

> "The effects of drunk driving put teens at a higher risk than adult drinkers because they definitely do not know their alcohol tolerance limit."[42]
>
> — AlcoholAlert.com.

How Much Is Too Much?

Among teens who drink, many do not realize just how many drinks will make them legally drunk. According to the website AlcoholAlert.com, this can cause serious trouble. The site explains: "The effects of drunk driving put teens at a higher risk than adult drinkers because they definitely do not know their alcohol tolerance limit. . . . An example would be the designated driver who is

Buying the Right Behavior

A group called Mariah's Challenge is offering monetary incentives not to drink and drive. The group was founded in Montana by Jimm Kilmer, Chad Okrusch, and Leo McCarthy after their daughters were struck by a teenage drunk driver in 2007 while walking down a sidewalk. (McCarthy's fourteen-year-old daughter, Mariah, was killed; the others were seriously injured.) Mariah's Challenge asks young people under age twenty-one to pledge publicly that they will neither drink alcohol nor get in a car with someone who has been drinking it. If they can keep this pledge throughout their high school years, they can apply to receive $1,000 from the group's scholarship program. In announcing the challenge on the day of his daughter's funeral, McCarthy told teens, "If you stick with me for four years, don't use alcohol, don't use illicit drugs but give back to your community, work with your parents and talk to your parents, I'll be there with a bunch of other people to give you money." So far, the group has awarded a scholarship to more than 140 high school graduates across the United States.

Quoted in Jamie Gumbrecht, "What Sways Teens Not to Drink, Drive? Stories, Not Stats," CNN, October 10, 2012. www.cnn.com.

cajoled into having just a few drinks. When it is time to leave the party or bar, the designated driver has ingested less alcohol than the others, so they end up driving drunk."[42]

The site also reports: "Studies have shown it only takes three to four, 12-ounce beers to inebriate a 170 pound male and that an average sized woman can become intoxicated after only one to three of those same beers. These statistics may seem unbelievable, but they are accurate. In one hour, a person can become so disoriented they can cause a terrible crash if they drive."[43]

Experts also report that teens do not experience the signs

that they are becoming drunk until they already have a great deal of alcohol in their bodies. That is, they go from feeling mildly drunk to very drunk more abruptly than adults. According to the US Department of Health & Human Services (DHHS), "Differences between the adult brain and the brain of the maturing adolescent also may help to explain why many young drinkers are able to consume much larger amounts of alcohol than adults before experiencing the negative consequences of drinking, such as drowsiness, lack of coordination, and withdrawal/hangover effects."[44] But even when teens are not feeling very drunk, experts say, their ability to drive well and respond quickly in emergencies is still seriously compromised.

Teen Education Programs

Nonetheless, many teens continue to think it is okay to drive while mildly drunk. To show how serious it can be to drive with any alcohol at all in one's system, various organizations have created programs for anti–drunk driving education targeted specifically at teens. Among these programs, the most widespread is Every 15 Minutes, which tries to re-create what it would be like to be involved in a fatal crash. The group states: "Life's lessons are best learned through experience. Unfortunately, when the target audience is teens and the topic is drinking and texting while driving, experience is not the teacher of choice. The Every 15 Minutes Program offers real-life experience without the real-life risks."[45]

To accomplish this, the two-day nationwide program begins by sending someone into high school classrooms to remove one student every fifteen minutes. This represents the fact that when the program was first created in the 1990s, it was estimated that in North America someone died from an alcohol-related collision every fifteen minutes. (Today that figure is estimated at every thirty to forty minutes.) The students designated as crash victims have been preselected, and they and their parents contribute to subsequent events. For example, the parents write an obituary that is read to classrooms

"Life's lessons are best learned through experience. Unfortunately, when the target audience is teens and the topic is drinking and texting while driving, experience is not the teacher of choice."[45]

— Every 15 Minutes.

Getting a Buzz

Surveys show that many teens have misconceptions about alcohol consumption. One of the most common is that drinking beer is safer than drinking other types of alcoholic beverages. Beer has a lower percentage of alcohol in it—between 4.2 and 5 percent, in comparison to 12 to 17 percent for wine and roughly 40 percent for liquor (distilled spirits). However, the bodily and sensory changes that accompany alcohol consumption—including the buzz (sense of euphoria) and loss of inhibition that many teen drinkers seek—only occurs after the person's blood alcohol content has reached the level of intoxication. This means that beer drinkers seeking a buzz will have to consume more drinks to achieve that than someone drinking wine or liquor. Moreover, because a state of intoxication depends on the percentage of alcohol in a person's body, a large person will take longer to get drunk than a small one. Because of this, laws use alcohol percentages in the bloodstream to identify whether someone is legally drunk. For example, in California an adult is legally drunk when his or her blood alcohol content reaches 0.8 percent, a number that many other states use for their legal limit as well.

upon the chosen student's "death," and afterward the student returns to the classroom in makeup intending to make him or her look dead. For the rest of the day, these "dead" students roam the school without interacting with anyone in any way.

The program also involves a crash scene simulation. On the afternoon of the first day, students view the wreckage of the crash where their classmates "died," and as part of this simulation, rescue workers treat student participants who are made up to look injured. Sometimes those involved in the fake crash have to be extricated by the jaws-of-life device that firefighters and paramedics use to free victims trapped in a wreck. In addition, a coroner is on the scene to handle the bodies of those who have supposedly died, and police officers are there to arrest and take away the student posing as the drunk driver who caused the crash. On the second day of the program, students attend an assembly where convicted drunk drivers, victims of drunk drivers, and professionals who deal with the aftermath of drunk driving crashes talk about their experiences.

Powerful Results

Originally Every 15 Minutes was only a one-day program, but as its use spread, highway patrol agencies began providing grant money to expand it. Soon it was addressing not only drunk driving but driving while under the influence of drugs. In recent years it has addressed the problem of driving while texting as well.

Surveys of participants both pre- and post-event suggest that the program has been effective in changing students' driving habits. For example, students who have been through the program are less likely to drive while drinking, drive after having had three to five or more drinks, or get into a car with a drunk driver behind the wheel. Students are also more likely to worry about how much their friends are drinking, more likely to have a designated non-drinking driver when going out in a group, more likely to call their parents for a ride home after they have been drinking, and more likely not to drink at all.

Teens who go through the program typically speak of how emotionally powerful it is. For example, at the Every 15 Minutes website, a participant named Mimi wrote in the site's guestbook: "It's incredibly emotional, especially for those of us who [have] lost a friend or family member to drunk driving or texting while driving (either in real life or they 'died' in this mock up.) It's even emotional that one of my friends was chosen as the 'walking dead.' Knowing she could be one in every 15 minutes still makes me cry. Thanks for having this. I think teens in general underestimate statistics, especial[ly] when it comes to drinking/texting while driving."[46]

Too Upsetting

Indeed, the program is typically the most effective in schools where a student has previously been killed or seriously injured as a result of drunk driving. However, some people have criticized it as being too upsetting for teens. Therapist Cynthia Brody of Lamorinda, California, is one such person. Some of her clients are teens who have been through the program, and their reactions to it have led her to complain about its severity and to call on parents of her community to think twice before giving their children permission to participate. She says:

> I have had kids tell me they were upset for a week, highly anxious and too distracted to focus on their studies after experiencing what felt like a real trauma. . . . I believe there are other ways of making the point that driving drunk is very dangerous. What bothers me most is that kids who have not been told about how this works begin crying and panicking when they realize friends are missing after the announcement is made that some of their peers have been killed in a car accident. Then, the screaming and death enacted and the body bags, morgue, friends in caskets and parents falling apart seems too much like instilling trauma unnecessarily to me. If it were parents staging something horrible to get a kid's attention they could be brought up on charges of emotional abuse.[47]

Effects Wear Off

Moreover, some experts believe that Every 15 Minutes and similar programs are not as effective as many people think. Studies have shown that for seven months after participating in the program, teens do have an increased tendency to avoid alcohol and to refrain from driving drunk. After this, however, for many teens the effect on behavior wears off, although these teens might still profess that they neither engage in nor support drinking and driving.

In fact, expert James C. Fell, senior program director at the Alcohol, Policy, and Safety Research Center in Calverton, Maryland, says there is no evidence that programs involving simulated

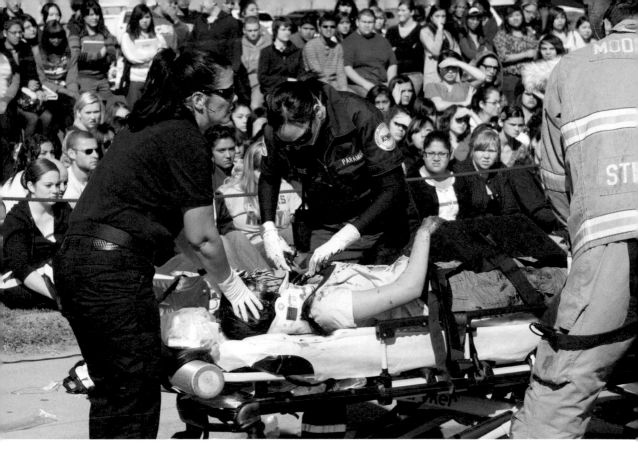

crashes change teens' attitudes in the long term. He says, "Mock crashes and emotional assemblies, I'm not against them. They're a temporary fix."[48] However, some experts say this short-term effect can still be used to prevent deaths from drunk driving, by holding such programs just prior to events like prom night and spring break that typically involve teen drinking.

Stories, Not Statistics

Research has also shown that one aspect of anti–drunk driving programs does seem to have a more long-lasting effect than the rest: the personal stories of those who have experienced a tragedy because of a drunk driving crash. After years of attempting to change attitudes about drunk driving, the organization Mothers Against Drunk Driving (MADD) has noted that school assemblies do not work nearly as well in terms of changing teen behavior as putting a face on warnings and statistics, especially when the face is that of a peer. For example, seventeen-year-old

At a mock car accident scene staged by the Every 15 Minutes program, high school students in Modesto, California, watch as a paramedic treats an injured patient. The program graphically illustrates the outcome of accidents involving teen drunk drivers.

Melissa Stegner, who has spoken at MADD events about how her family was killed by a drunk driver in 2007, has been successful at influencing the attitudes of other teens in regard to drunk driving. She says, "I remind my friends that no matter what, drinking and driving is not OK. There's no dumber decision you can make. . . . I've had people come up to me and thank me."[49]

MADD has found that parents also have influence over their teens' behavior in regard to alcohol use. The national president of the group, Jan Withers, says, "Parents believe the peer pressure is so great that they don't have as much influence on their teens as they actually do." She adds that if parents feel empowered to address the issue, "it moves into the power of community—students and adults work together."[50]

Reason for Concern

Indeed, in many places where communities, parents, and teachers have come together to reinforce the message that drunk driving is unacceptable, drunk driving rates among teens have gone down. In October 2012 a report by the CDC revealed that teen drinking and driving rates had dropped by 54 percent over the previous twenty years. Many adults find this encouraging.

However, the report also offered some reason for concern. Roughly 1 million teens drank and drove in 2011, and one in ten admits to drinking and driving at least once a month. In addition, 85 percent of high schoolers who admit to drinking and driving have done so at least once after binge drinking, which the CDC defines as having at least five alcoholic drinks within just a few hours.

Moreover, there will always be teens who ignore warnings about the dangers of drunk driving no matter how these warnings are presented. For example, Davonne Lawson of Harrisburg, Pennsylvania, who participated in an Every 15 Minutes program at his high school when he was nineteen, ignored its message entirely. When a speaker talked about about how drunk driving could destroy lives, Lawson says, "I just looked at

"I remind my friends that no matter what, drinking and driving is not OK. There's no dumber decision you can make."[49]

— Melissa Stegner, whose family was killed by a teenage drunk driver.

him like, this would never be me."[51] However, a few months later Lawson drove drunk, tried to pass a car in his way, and crashed into and killed a motorcyclist. He was sentenced to three to seven years in jail, during which he was allowed to go out into the community periodically to speak out against drunk driving. While he accepts the consequences of his own actions, he also says that one of the reasons he drove drunk was peer pressure from the "wrong crowd." He adds, "I know now where that life gets me."[52]

The Wrong Crowd

"The wrong crowd" to which Lawson refers—that is, teens who behave recklessly and encourage others to do the same—is a group with certain shared tendencies that encourage alcohol abuse. The DHHS reports:

> Young people who are disruptive, hyperactive, and ag-gressive—often referred to as having conduct problems or being antisocial—as well as those who are depressed, withdrawn, or anxious, may be at greatest risk for alcohol problems. Other behavior problems associated with alco-hol use include rebelliousness, difficulty avoiding harm or harmful situations, and a host of other traits seen in young people who act out without regard for rules or the feelings of others (i.e., disinhibition).[53]

Such teens are also likely to have poor relationships with their parents, which makes it difficult for them to call for a ride home when they drink too much to drive, and a lack of parental supervi-sion, which makes it easier for them to drink illegally. Without a supportive home life, they are more likely to be influenced by and to want to fit in with their friends. For many of these teens, it takes an extreme experience such as Lawson's to get them to change their behaviors. "What I'm trying to get people to know," he says in dis-cussing his talks to teens, "is you don't have to go through anything tragic"[54] in order to learn the dangers of drinking and driving.

Facts

- The NHTSA uses the word "crash" instead of "accident" to refer to alcohol-related vehicle crashes in order to highlight the fact that these events are foreseeable and therefore preventable rather than accidental.

- SADD (Students Against Destructive Decisions) reports that in a December 2012 survey, nearly 50 percent of teenage drivers in the United States considered driving on New Year's Eve to be extremely dangerous, yet 12 percent admit to having driven under the influence of alcohol or drugs on New Year's Eve.

- According to SADD, 47 percent of teens say their parents allow them to go to parties where alcohol is served; 15 percent of teens say their parents allow them to throw parties where alcohol is served; and 29 percent of teens say that their parents allow them to drink unsupervised.

- According to the anti–drunk driving group Mariah's Challenge, 45 percent of those who die in car crashes involving a drunk driver under the age of twenty-one are people other than the driver.

- According to the CDC, by the time of the average drunk driver's first arrest, he or she has already driven drunk eighty times.

CHAPTER FIVE

Are More Laws Needed to Fight Distracted Driving?

In December 2011 the NTSB called for a nationwide ban on the use of all cell phones, handheld and hands-free, and any other form of texting device while driving. Only phone devices integrated into the car and operated by voice controls, the NTSB said, should be excluded from the ban. NTSB member Robert Sumwalt referred to driving under the influence of alcohol, or DUI, when he said that such a drastic step was necessary because distracted driving "is becoming the new DUI. It's becoming epidemic."[55]

At the time of this call to action, laws on cell phone use while driving were being decided by individual states. Thirty states had decided to make it illegal for novice drivers to use cell phones, and thirty-five to ban text messaging while driving. However, only ten had banned the use of all handheld phones while driving. Moreover, states varied in the aggressiveness with which they enforced these laws.

NTSB chairwoman Barbara Deborah Hersman said that the increasing popularity of smartphones, which have so many distracting features, has made it necessary to be more aggressive in addressing the problem. She acknowledged that a ban on all cell phones will inconvenience people. "Needless lives are lost on our highways, and for what?" she says. "Convenience? Death isn't convenient. So we can stay more connected? A fatal accident severs that connection."[56]

Do Bans Work?

To date, however, no such national ban has been enacted, and people continue to disagree on whether it is a worthwhile approach to solving the problem of distracted driving. Some of this resistance to enactment is due to the fact that the legislation would have a major impact on drivers who are heavy cell phone users, particularly if the ban ever spreads to include hands-free phones as well as handheld ones. But the resistance is also due to the fact that studies suggest such bans might not have the desired effects.

For example, a 2010 study by the Highway Loss Data Institute (HLDI) found no reduction in crashes in four states after a texting ban took effect. Adrian Lund, president of both HLDI and the Insurance Institute for Highway Safety, reports: "Texting bans haven't reduced crashes at all. In a perverse twist, crashes increased in 3 of the 4 states we studied after bans were enacted. It's an indication that texting bans might even increase the risk of texting for drivers who continue to do so despite the laws."[57]

Experts are unsure why this increase might be occurring. However, Lund speculates that bans cause drivers to hide their texting by holding their phones lower in their laps, which in turn makes quick glances at the road while texting more difficult. In any case, he believes the problem with such laws lies in their specificity. "They're focusing on a single manifestation of distracted driving and banning it," he says. "This ignores the endless sources of distraction and relies on banning one source or another to solve the whole problem."[58]

Results Not Uniform

Another study suggests that the one-size-fits-all approach to such laws means that they do not work uniformly well across the country. Reported by the University of Illinois in November 2012, this

> "Needless lives are lost on our highways, and for what? Convenience? Death isn't convenient. So we can stay more connected? A fatal accident severs that connection."[56]

— NTSB chairwoman Barbara Deborah Hersman on the use of smartphones.

DON'T LET TEXTING BLIND YOU

STOP THE TEXTS. STOP THE WRECKS.

study shows that banning cell phones has a different effect in rural areas than in cities. Researchers examined seven years' worth of crash data from New York, where cell phone use while driving was banned in 2002, and Pennsylvania, which had no such ban. They found that over time, cell phone bans reduced personal injury accidents in cities but had no statistically significant effect in rural areas. In fact, in very rural areas, there was a relative increase in accident rates over the seven-year period.

Consequently Douglas King, a coauthor of the study, says, "What we found in our research is that the cellphone ban was associated with different outcomes in different groups of counties. Based on this research, it suggests that a blanket cellphone ban may not always lead to a greater benefit. Based on the seven-year time period . . . the outcome in each group of counties after the ban was not uniformly beneficial." However, King adds, "This is the kind of research that definitely should encourage densely populated areas to enact these laws. There's sufficient evidence to support it. When you start getting into rural and very rural areas, I think you have to have to take it in a case-by-case basis. But for urban areas, the evidence is substantial."[59]

A Broader Ban

Some experts have suggested that since cities have more traffic accidents than do rural areas, it does not take much of a reduction

A billboard in Washington DC urges teens to not text and drive. Public service campaigns paired with the adoption of laws in states around the country are part of an effort to fight distracted driving.

in accident rates to make it seem like a big improvement has occurred. Others have suggested that because cities typically have more law enforcement officers per mile driven, city drivers are more reluctant than rural ones to flout driving laws. That is, perhaps the reason the accident rates did not go down in rural areas after a ban was enacted was because many drivers there were ignoring the ban and not getting caught.

Experts say that the success of a ban depends largely on how aggressively it is enforced. In California, for example, where a ban on using handheld cell phones while driving has been enforced aggressively since July 2008, deaths caused by drivers using handheld cell phones dropped 47 percent. Enforcement programs targeting cell phone use in New York and Connecticut in 2011 had similar success. In Hartford, Connecticut, for example, talking on a handheld cell phone while driving dropped 57 percent and texting while driving dropped 72 percent during the period when law enforcement officers were aggressively pulling over and ticketing drivers seen using a handheld phone behind the wheel.

However, Jonathan Adkins, spokesman for the Governors Highway Safety Association, notes that the key to such successes is to convince people not to engage in the behavior in the first place. He says, "The public has to believe they are going to get a ticket if they do this while they're driving. You have to have signs up, you have to have aggressive enforcement, and you have to let people know you're enforcing it. . . . The goal isn't to write tickets; the goal is to change behavior."[60]

"The goal isn't to write tickets; the goal is to change behavior."[60]

— Jonathan Adkins of the Governors Highway Safety Association.

Education Programs

Some experts say that the way to change behavior is not by making people afraid of getting a ticket. This fear often wanes when individuals discover they can indulge in the behavior without getting caught. Indeed, it is difficult for police officers to spot someone texting because the device is often held too low for it to be seen through car windows and can be hidden if the officer pulls the driver over for some other infraction. Fernando Wilson of the

University of North Texas Health Science Center, an expert on cell phone use while driving, notes, "Unlike drunk driving, where you have effective enforcement mechanisms you don't have that with texting. The cop just has to get lucky and see you texting while driving."[61]

With enforcement difficult, then, some experts say the best way to change behavior is not through laws but through education programs. In June 2012 the US Department of Transportation supported this approach by launching pilot programs designed to teach young drivers about the dangers of distracted driving. Part of an overall "blueprint" for curbing distracted driving, these education programs partner the NHTSA with driver education professionals in order to update the standard curriculum for teens learning the rules of the road. Ellen Bloom, a director of federal policy, says, "We've learned that the number-one way to convince young drivers to stop texting behind the wheel is to educate them on just how deadly the risks are, and that's a big part of this blueprint by the Transportation Department."[62]

The blueprint also includes finding ways to encourage high school students to spread the message among friends and family that distracted driving is dangerous. The NHTSA is charged with raising awareness among parents as well, so that they will establish rules for their teens that reduce distracted driving, and with encouraging teachers to participate in this process. At the same time, the blueprint addresses the need for continuing aggressive law enforcement and calls on any state that has not already banned texting while driving to do so.

> "The cop just has to get lucky and see you texting while driving."[61]
>
> — Fernando Wilson of the University of North Texas Health Science Center.

Mixed Messages

Some experts, however, say that state laws are weakening the message that it is not okay to use a cell phone to talk or to text while driving. California, for example, prohibits these activities while driving—except when hands-free technology is involved. At first this was only the case with talking while driving, but in January 2013 a new law went into effect allowing adult drivers to use hands-free technology to send and read text messages while driving. This

Cracking Down on Alcohol Servers

To help reduce teenage drunk driving, states have passed laws that severely punish bar owners and employees who illegally sell teenagers alcohol. The first use of such a law in Douglas County, Nebraska, was in December 2012, when an employee at the Fire Barn Bar was charged with a felony for serving alcohol to two teens who were subsequently in a car accident. The server, twenty-year-old Amanda Heiman, knew the two were underage and also knew that the bar had refused to serve them earlier in the day after seeing their IDs. But eighteen-year-old Jacob Dickmeyer and nineteen-year-old Colby Burke were her friends, so she provided them with two pitchers of beer and six other alcoholic drinks during the course of the evening. She then loaned them her car so they could drive home because their ride had not shown up. En route, at around 1:15 a.m., they lost control of the car while speeding and crashed. Burke survived with serious injuries, but Dickmeyer was thrown from the car and died at the scene. Heiman is facing a sentence of five years in prison or five years on probation.

means it is legal for adult drivers to compose messages by voice on a smartphone, for example, and verify the message's accuracy by glancing at the display, as long as they are not holding the device.

Another new law in the state seems to encourage drivers to have their cell phones at the ready at all times. As of January 2013, if a police officer pulls a driver over for a ticket and asks for proof of automobile insurance and registration, the driver is allowed to provide this proof via an electronic device such as a smartphone or tablet. Law enforcement officers say this will make the verification process easier for both officers and drivers. But critics point out that the NTSB has specifically recommended banning the use of tablets in a motor vehicle, and a few states already prohibit young drivers from using any handheld device while behind the wheel. (Although typically for devices other than a cellphone—e.g., a video game device or an iPad—the law states that the driver cannot be cited simply for using the device but must have first been pulled over for unsafe driving.)

Hands-Free Exclusions

Indeed, some experts say that the only devices that should be allowed in a motor vehicle are those necessary to operate the vehicle safely. They were therefore disappointed when the NTSB excluded hands-free devices from its January 2012 call on all states to ban drivers from using any portable electronic devices (sometimes referred to simply as PEDs) while operating a motor vehicle. These devices would include not only cell phones but GPS devices, iPads, MP3 players, and other handheld devices, but not controls related to hands-free operation, such as headsets.

In support of this exclusion, US transportation secretary Ray LaHood says, "The problem is not hands-free. That is not the big problem in America."[63] But studies suggest that the voice controls of a hands-free phone can be as distracting as a handheld phone because of how they affect cognition. Moreover, hands-free phones can pose a physical distraction whenever they require a headset since, as Richard Read explains, this headset is "really just another device liable to fall to the floorboard"[64] for drivers to pick up. Nonetheless, no state seems eager to ban the use of hands-free phones for all drivers.

Broad Laws

There are also no specific bans against eating while driving, but some lawmakers are considering them. This is the case, for example, with the city council in Bowling Green, Ohio. Unhappy that their state's anti-texting law does not go further in addressing the problem of distracted driving, council members crafted a law saying that drivers had to give "full time and attention to the operation of the vehicle."[65] Critics of the law say that it is far too broad, making it possible for police to ticket drivers simply for taking a sip of water. However, councilman Robert McComber says, "This isn't about banning people from eating or drinking while driving, but preventing them from trying to do both while steering the car with their knees or thighs."[66]

The Ohio law is an example of legislation that prohibits distracted driving in general as opposed to specific activities and devices. These laws prohibit a driver from doing anything that results in the vehicle being operated in an unsafe way. As of February 2013 four states had anti–distracted driving laws: Idaho, Maine, South Carolina, and Utah. The District of Columbia also specifically prohibits distracted driving, which it defines as inattentive driving while operating a motor vehicle. In addition, while Hawaii has no law at the state level to address distracted driving in general, all of its counties have such a law, and the state specifically bans talking or texting on a cell phone while driving.

However, as in Ohio, wherever anti–distracted driving laws are proposed, critics say they must be carefully worded in order to prevent abuse. As John Bowman, spokesman for the National Motorists Association, says, "Distracted driving takes place when a driver exhibits clear behavior that is either hazardous or shows recklessness on the road, so it needs to be defined."[67] But Bowman adds that he believes police should not ticket drivers for breaking these laws but merely warn them not to do it again. His group argues that education rather than more laws is the way to deal with the problem of distracted driving.

Technology Can Help

Russ Rader of the Insurance Institute for Highway Safety in Arlington, Virginia, shares this opposition to new laws. However, he does not agree that more education is the solution, because studies have shown that many drivers are well-educated about the dangers of distracting behavior and yet engage in them anyway. Consequently Rader points to new technology as the key to reducing distracted driving. This is because, he believes, there are too many behaviors to legislate, and it is impossible for law

"This isn't about banning people from eating or drinking while driving, but preventing them from trying to do both while steering the car with their knees or thighs."[66]

— Councilman Robert McComber on the Bowling Green, Ohio, proposal for a new distracted driving law.

enforcement officers to catch drivers every time they engage in a dangerous behavior.

"New laws are not likely the answer," he says. He adds that there is "the potential for technology to help bring drivers' attention back to the road at critical moments, no matter what is distracting them, whether they're reaching for a cup of coffee, trying to send a text message or just daydreaming."[68] As an example of such technology, Rader cites a vehicle feature whereby it brakes automatically whenever it senses a person or object in its path.

There are also features that ensure that drivers will not use in-car devices at the wrong time. For example, some GPS devices installed in vehicles will not be programmable when the vehicle is moving. Similarly, some people have called for the development of a device that would be installed in every car to jam cell phone signals so that cell phones would stop transmitting, thereby preventing talking or texting while driving.

In many states the laws allow drivers to talk on their phones as long as they use hands-free devices. Some research has found that carrying on a phone conversation is a serious distraction whether the driver is holding the phone or using a hands-free device.

Experts say there are also less dramatic ways to reduce distracted driving through technology. One of the simplest is to change the typefaces used to display information on devices. In a September 2012 study of device screen displays in cars, researchers from the Massachusetts Institute of Technology AgeLab, the New England University Transportation Center, and the Monotype Imaging Holdings (which provides typefaces to devices) found that certain changes in typeface style reduced how long drivers glanced at the devices by as much as 10 percent.

Unintended Results

Sometimes, however, a new technology created to address problems related to distracted driving can have unintended results. For example, experts have long known that using an MP3 player like the iPod to play music while driving can increase the risk of an accident. In fact, a study in 2009 found that using an MP3 device while driving was more dangerous than talking on a cell phone. Consequently manufacturers of MP3s have developed supplementary technology that they believe makes the devices less distracting.

Unfortunately, what was intended to reduce driver distractions actually appears to increase them. This was one of the findings of a study released in April 2012 by researchers from the University of Wisconsin–Madison. The study was designed to discover, among other things, whether a supplementary device designed to adapt a portable MP3 for use in the car lived up to claims that it made the MP3 less distracting.

The MP3 used in this study was a fifth-generation iPod with a small color screen, mounted on the dashboard of a driving simulator. This docking station was one part of the supplementary device; the other part was a controller whereby users could scroll, or advance quickly, through a playlist of songs. This controller was down at the right side of the driver's seat, so that when the driver's right arm was at rest the controller was easily in reach.

Test subjects were told to scroll through alphabetically sorted playlists of 20, 75, or 580 songs to find a specific song, using both the controller and an ordinary handheld iPod. The researchers measured how long it took them to do this, how long their eyes

Facebooking While Driving

On January 14, 2012, eighteen-year-old Taylor Sauer updated her Facebook status to read: "I can't discuss this now. Driving and facebooking is not safe! Haha." While writing this, she was making a four-hour, late-night drive on Interstate 84 from Utah State University in Logan, Utah, to her parents' home in Caldwell, Idaho. She was also using her cell phone to exchange Facebook and text messages with friends, even at speeds of over 80 miles per hour (129 kph). The road was flat until she reached a hill that a tanker trunk was struggling to climb at 15 miles per hour (24 kph). Just moments after she updated her Facebook status, Sauer rear-ended the truck and died in the crash.

Police later learned that Sauer had not applied her brakes before hitting the truck. They also estimated that she had been sending a message every ninety seconds while driving, and she received numerous messages as well, many as part of a back-and-forth conversation with a friend about the Denver Broncos. After Sauer's death her parents theorized that she had been engaging in this behavior in order to stay awake, but they went before the media to call on the state of Idaho to ban texting and facebooking while driving.

were off the road, how often they had to glance back and forth in order to accomplish the task, and how they reacted to different driving conditions while doing this. The researchers also compared this new technology with old technology by having test subjects also tune a car radio to a specific frequency.

This study showed that the controller actually increased distraction in comparison with using a handheld iPod. Test subjects looked at the controller for longer periods and glanced at it more frequently. In addition, whether with the controller or the iPod itself, the longer the playlist the longer the driver failed to pay attention to the road, even though the driver was only charged with finding one song on the list. Moreover, tuning the radio proved to be less of a distraction than using an MP3 player, leading the researchers to conclude that scrolling while driving is more dangerous than selecting a station on a car stereo.

The head of the study, John Lee, says, "New technology in the car often seems like familiar old technology, such as a radio, but is often much more likely to distract."[69] Consequently he advises that new technologies not be promoted as being safer than existing technologies until they have been thoroughly tested. Others argue that drivers do not need any new technologies, given that existing ones are causing enough accidents as it is.

A Boring Activity

In fact, some suggest that cell phones should be banned from cars altogether, much the way open containers of alcohol are banned from being carried in cars, at least for teen drivers. But others say that it is far easier to prevent the majority of teens from drinking while driving than it is to prevent them from using technology while driving, simply because of the nature of driving. As technology expert Ed Hardy notes:

> As much as Americans say we like to drive, if you think about, really think about it, it's actually a completely boring activity. How exciting is it to drive back and forth to the office for the thousandth time? How thrilling is it to work your way through rush hour traffic to the grocery store? If you find driving exciting, you're probably not doing it right. It's so dull we are often tempted to pull out our phones and start texting or checking *Twitter* while we're doing it.[70]

Given that this is the case, even new laws and aggressive enforcement will probably not keep teens from being tempted to reach for a distraction, ignoring the risk of what might happen when they do.

Facts

- The US government has declared April to be National Distracted Driving Awareness Month.

- Ninety percent of new vehicles sold in the United States offer buyers iPod connectivity.

- According to the NHTSA in 2012, at any given moment during daylight hours approximately 13.5 million drivers are using a handheld cell phone.

- According to the NHTSA, almost half of all adults own smartphones.

- According to the car-buying site Edmunds, about 99 percent of 2012 vehicles had standard or optional Bluetooth connectivity for phones with voice controls, and many vehicles had voice-controlled GPS systems as well.

- Thirty-nine states as well as the District of Columbia and Guam specifically ban text messaging for all drivers, and ten states, the District of Columbia, and the Virgin Islands prohibit all drivers from using handheld cell phones while driving.

Source Notes

Introduction: Dangerous Driving

1. Quoted in Dave Collins (Associated Press), "Connecticut Teen Driver, Said to Be Using Cellphone, Is Charged in Jogger's Death," *Columbus Dispatch*, May 15, 2012. www.dispatch.com.

2. Quoted in *Stamford Advocate*, "Woman Wants Stricter Distracted Driving Laws," February 4, 2013. www.stamfordadvocate.com.

3. Quoted in Hands-Free Info, "New Jersey: Cell Phone Laws, Legislation," February 22, 2013. http://handsfreeinfo.com.

4. Quoted in Hands-Free Info, "New Jersey: Cell Phone Laws, Legislation."

5. Distraction.gov, Official US Government Website of Distracted Driving, "What Is Distracted Driving?" www.distraction.gov.

6. Quoted in Josh Max, "Distracted Driving Risks Largely Ignored by Youngsters," *New York Daily News*, April 30, 2012. www.nydailynews.com.

Chapter One: What Are the Origins of Concerns About Teen Driving Habits?

7. Quoted in Ashley Halsey III, "Nighttime Driving Is the Biggest Danger for Teen Drivers, Study Says," *Washington Post*, May 6, 2010. www.washingtonpost.com.

8. Amanda Lenhart, Rich Ling, Scott Campbell, and Kristen Purcell, "Teens and Mobile Phones," Pew Internet and American Life Project, April 20, 2010. http://pewinternet.org.

9. Quoted in Shane McGlaun, "Scientific Study Links 16,000 Deaths to Texting and Talking While Driving," *Daily Tech*, September 24, 2010. www.dailytech.com.

10. Jarad Dewing, "The Cold Slab and the Razor: My Old Faith, Gone Beyond Resurrection," Gawker, February 16, 2013. http://gawker.com.

Chapter Two: How Do Cell Phones Affect Teen Driving Habits?

11. Quoted in Ally Donnelly, "Prosecution: Aaron Deveau Deleted Texts Following Crash," NECN News, May 29, 2012. www.necn .com.

12. Quoted in Brian R. Ballou and John R. Ellement, "Haverhill Teen to Serve Year in Jail for Fatal Texting Crash; Judge Calls for People to Keep Eyes on Road," *Boston Globe*, June 6, 2012. www.boston.com.

13. Quoted in Ballou and Ellement, "Haverhill Teen to Serve Year in Jail for Fatal Texting Crash."

14. Quoted in Anzellotti Sperling Pazol and Small, "Toddler Killed by Texting Driver," blog. http://aspands.com.

15. David L. Strayer and Frank A. Drews, "Cell-Phone-Induced Driver Distraction," *Current Directions in Psychological Science*, vol. 16, no. 3, 2007, p. 128.

16. Strayer and Drews, "Cell-Phone-Induced Driver Distraction," p. 129.

17. Quoted in Jim Forsyth, "Texting While Driving More Dangerous than Thought," Reuters, October 5, 2011. http://www.reuters.com.

18. Michael Austin, "Texting While Driving: How Dangerous Is It?" *Car and Driver*, June 2009. www.caranddriver.com.

19. Austin, "Texting While Driving: How Dangerous Is It?"

20. Phil LeBeau, "Texting and Driving Worse than Drinking and Driving," CNBC, June 25, 2009. www.cnbc.com.

21. LeBeau, "Texting and Driving Worse than Drinking and Driving."

22. Timothy Geigner, "Shocking Revelation: It Isn't the Phone That's Dangerous; It's the Driver," Techdirt.com, August 27, 2012. www .techdirt.com.

23. Nan Zhao, Bryan Reimer, Bruce Mehler, Lisa A. D'Ambrosio, and Joseph F. Coughlin, "Self-Reported and Observed Risky Driving Behaviors Among Frequent and Infrequent Cell Phone Users," abstract, ScienceDirect. www.sciencedirect.com.

24. Quoted in Carol Cruzan Morton, "Why Cell Phone Bans Don't Work," *Science*, August 22, 2012. http://news.sciencemag.org.

25. Geigner, "Shocking Revelation."

Chapter Three: Are Teen Drivers More Susceptible to Distractions?

26. RAC, "Young Drivers Suffer from Overconfidence," January 25, 2009. http://rac.com.au.

27. PEMCO, "The Psychology of Teenage Driving." www.pemco.com.

28. Quoted in Brad Gerick, "Coffee Spill Causes Constant Friendship Cliff Car Crash," *BelAirPatch*, October 5, 2011. http://belair.patch .com.

29. Tim Hollister, "Should Teen Drivers Use Global Positioning Systems?," *From Reid's Dad* (blog), August 22, 2010. http://fromreids dad.org.

30. Quoted in Amanda Gardener, "Most US Drivers Engage in 'Distracting' Behaviors," *USA Today*, December 1, 2011. http://usatoday 30.usatoday.com.

31. University of North Carolina Highway Safety Research Center, "Why Are Young Drivers at a Greater Risk?" www.hsrc.unc.edu.

32. National Safety Council, "Understanding the Distracted Brain," white paper, March 2010. www.nsc.org.

33. National Safety Council, "Understanding the Distracted Brain."

34. Quoted in *NewsHour*, "Cell Phone Use Raises Risks While Driving, Studies Show," transcript, PBS, July 28, 2009. www.pbs.org.

35. Richard Read, "Survey Says: Younger Drivers Prone to Get Lost, Frustrated," Car Connection, August 8, 2011. www.thecarconnec tion.com.

36. Quoted in Larry Copeland, "Teen Driver Risks in High Gear over Summer," *USA Today*, June 21, 2010. http://usatoday30.usatoday .com.

37. Quoted in Copeland, "Teen Driver Risks in High Gear over Summer."

Chapter Four: How Can Teens Be Convinced Not to Drink and Drive?

38. Quoted in Horace Holmes and Tom Roussey, "University Boulevard Accident Kills Two Women, Injures Another," ABC7 News, December 29, 2011. www.wjla.com.

39. Andrea McCarren, "Desaleen James Shares Her Story and Video from the Driving Crash That Killed Her Two Friends," WUSA9 News, May 8, 2012. www.wusa9.com.

40. McCarren, "Desaleen James Shares Her Story and Video from the Driving Crash That Killed Her Two Friends."

41. McCarren, "Desaleen James Shares Her Story and Video from the Driving Crash That Killed Her Two Friends."

42. AlcoholAlert.com, "The Real Effects of Drunk Driving." www.alcohol alert.com.

43. AlcoholAlert.com, "The Real Effects of Drunk Driving."

44. US Department of Health & Human Services, National Institutes of Health, National Institute on Alcohol Abuse and Alcoholism, "Alcohol Alert: Underage Drinking," January 2006. http://pubs.niaaa.nih.gov.

45. Every 15 Minutes, "About Us." www.every15minutes.com.

46. Mimi, Guestbook, Every 15 Minutes. www.every15minutes.com.

47. Cynthia Brody, "Every 15 Minutes Program: Helpful or Too Traumatic?," Lamorinda Patch, October 22, 2011. http://lamorinda.patch.com.

48. Quoted in Central Valley Moms, "Prom Time Mock Accidents Give Teens a Dose of Reality About Drinking and Driving, but Do the Lessons Stick?," Central Valley Moms, June 7, 2010. http://centralvalleymoms.com.

49. Quoted in Jamie Gumbrecht, "What Sways Teens Not to Drink, Drive? Stories, Not Stats," CNN, October 10, 2012. www.cnn.com.

50. Quoted in Gumbrecht, "What Sways Teens Not to Drink, Drive? Stories, Not Stats.

51. Quoted in Central Valley Moms, "Prom Time Mock Accidents Give Teens a Dose of Reality About Drinking and Driving, but Do the Lessons Stick?"

52. Quoted in Central Valley Moms, "Prom Time Mock Accidents Give Teens a Dose of Reality About Drinking and Driving, but Do the Lessons Stick?"

53. US Department of Health & Human Services, National Institutes of Health, National Institute on Alcohol Abuse and Alcoholism, "Alcohol Alert: Underage Drinking."

54. Quoted in Central Valley Moms, "Prom Time Mock Accidents Give Teens a Dose of Reality About Drinking and Driving, but Do the Lessons Stick?"

Chapter Five: Are More Laws Needed to Fight Distracted Driving?

55. Quoted in Mike M. Ahlers, "NTSB Recommends Full Ban on Cell Phones While Driving," CNN, December 14, 2011. www.cnn.com.

56. Quoted in Ahlers, "NTSB Recommends Full Ban on Cell Phones While Driving."

57. Highway Loss Data Institute, "Texting Bans Don't Reduce Crashes; Effects are Slight Crash Increases," news release, September 28, 2010. www.iihs.org.

58. Highway Loss Data Institute, "Texting Bans Don't Reduce Crashes."

59. Quoted in e! Science News, "Study: Cellphone Bans Associated with Fewer Urban Accidents," November 15, 2012. http://esciencenews.com.

60. Quoted in Jacob Mayer, "Amarillo's Cellphone Ordinance Could Be Difficult to Enforce," *Amarillo Globe News*, September 19, 2012. http://amarillo.com.

61. Quoted in Shane McGlaun, "Scientific Study Links 16,000 Deaths to Texting and Talking While Driving," September 24, 2010, *Daily Tech*. http://www.dailytech.com.

62. Quoted in *Consumer Reports*, "Government Unveils Blueprint for Curbing Distracted Driving, Announces New Pilot Programs," June 7, 2012. http://news.consumerreports.org.

63. Quoted in Richard Read, "True or False: Hands-Free Calls Are Safer than Hand-Held?," Car Connection, April 26, 2012. www.thecarconnection.com.

64. Quoted in Read, "True or False."

65. Quoted in Gary Gastelu, "Ohio City's Distracted Driving Law Could Restrict Eating, Drinking Behind the Wheel," Fox News, July 25, 2012. www.foxnews.com.

66. Quoted in Gastelu, "Ohio City's Distracted Driving Law."

67. Quoted in Gastelu, "Ohio City's Distracted Driving Law."

68. Quoted in Amanda Gardner, "Most U.S. Drivers Engage in 'Distracting' Behaviors," Healthday, *USA Today*, December 1, 2011. http://usatoday30.usatoday.com.

69. Quoted in HFES News, "MP3 Song-Searching Can Increase Risk for Drivers," Human Factors and Ergonomics Society, April 16, 2012. www.hfes.org.

70. Ed Hardy, "We Shouldn't Ban Cell Phones in Cars, We Should Ban Drivers," Brighthand Smartphone News & Reviews, December 16, 2011. www.brighthand.com.

Related Organizations and Websites

CellPhoneSafety.org

CellPhoneSafety.org was created by the National Consumer Advocacy Commission, which works to educate consumers on safety and economic issues surrounding certain products and services. The website concentrates on issues related to the safety and financial concerns of cell phone use.

CTIA—The Wireless Association

1400 Sixteenth St. NW, Suite 600
Washington, DC 20036
phone: (202) 736-3200
fax: (202) 785-0721

Founded in 1984, this international nonprofit membership organization supports the wireless communications industry and provides information on cell phone–related issues and laws.

Distracted Driving Foundation

phone: (206) 919-1798
e-mail: info@ddfn.org
website: www.ddfn.org

This group is working with technology providers, mobile carriers, and handset manufacturers to create technical solutions to the problem of distracted driving as it relates to talking and texting on cell phones.

Don't Drive and Text.org
222 N. Main St., Suite A
Bryan, TX 77803
website: http://dontdriveandtext.org

This organization provides information on the dangers of texting and driving as part of a campaign to stop the practice.

DrinkingAndDriving.org
18275 Grove Pl.
Fontana, CA 92336
phone: (888) 502-3236
website: www.drinkinganddriving.org

DrinkingAndDriving.org works to prevent drunk driving, especially among teens, through education and tools such as directories listing driving services that will drive home people who have been drinking.

Governors Highway Safety Association (GHSA)
444 North Capitol St. NW, Suite 722
Washington, DC 20001
phone: (202) 789-0942
website: www.ghsa.org

This nonprofit organization represents state and territorial highway safety offices involved in implementing programs and policies related to highway safety issues. To this end, it promotes traffic safety and advocates for efforts to improve traffic safety.

Mariah's Challenge
PO Box 66
Butte, MT 59703
phone: (406) 490-2739
website: www.mariahschallenge.com

Founded in Montana by three men whose daughters were struck by a teenage drunk driver, Mariah's Challenge asks young people under age twenty-one to pledge publicly that they will neither drink alcohol nor get into a car with someone who has been drinking it. Individuals who can keep this pledge throughout their high school years are eligible to receive $1,000 from the group's scholarship program.

Mothers Against Drunk Driving (MADD)

511 E. John Carpenter Fwy., Suite 700
Irving, TX 75062
phone: (877) 275-6233
website: www.madd.org

MADD is dedicated to stopping drunk driving, to supporting the victims of drunk driving accidents, and to preventing underage drinking.

National Highway Traffic Safety Administration (NHTSA)

1200 New Jersey Ave. SE
West Bldg.
Washington, DC 20590
phone: (888) 327-4236
website: www.nhtsa.gov

Established by the Highway Safety Act of 1970, this federal agency directs highway safety and consumer programs, works to help prevent crashes, and researches issues and recommends policies related to highway and vehicle safety.

National Organizations for Youth Safety

7371 Atlas Walk Way #109
Gainesville, VA 20155
website: www.noys.org

A collaboration of over seventy national youth-serving organizations, including nonprofit organizations, business and industry leaders, and government agencies, this organization promotes safe and healthy behaviors among young people in the United States.

To this end, it works to prevent such problems as teen drug abuse, school bullying, and teen driver distractions across the country.

Pew Research Center
1615 L St. NW, Suite 700
Washington, DC 20036
phone: (202) 419-4300
e-mail: info@pewresearch.org

The Pew Research Center is a nonpartisan research organization that provides information on a variety of issues, attitudes, and trends. Its Pew Internet & American Life Project specifically addresses the impact of the Internet on American life and society and has conducted studies related to cell phone use.

Students Against Destructive Decisions (SADD)
255 Main St.
Marlborough, MA 01752
phone: (844) 723-3462
website: www.sadd.org

The original mission of SADD, which has chapters across the United States, was to prevent drinking and driving among teens. However, it now addresses other issues related to teen safety as well, including distracted driving.

Text Free Driving Organization
website: www.textfreedriving.org

Based in Florida, this group is dedicated to raising awareness of the dangers of texting and working to support laws that would eliminate cell phone use while driving.

Texting Organization Against Distracted Driving (TOADD), Inc.
531 Forest Oak Dr.
Stockbridge, GA 30281
phone: (678) 428-0046
website: www.toadd.org

Since October 2010 this organization has been dedicated to improving safety related to mobile phone technology by addressing issues related to distracted driving as well as to sexting and cyberbullying.

United States Department of Transportation

1200 New Jersey Ave. SE
Washington, DC 20590
phone: (855) 368-4200
website: www.dot.gov

This government agency is charged with ensuring a safe, efficient, and convenient transportation system. As part of its efforts to improve driver, vehicle, and road safety it has been working toward combating distracted driving. The agency also provides information on distracted driving at a website dedicated to the issue, www. distraction.gov.

Additional Reading

Books

Stefan Kiesbye, *Cell Phones and Driving*. Farmington Hills, MI: Greenhaven, 2011.

Stefan Kiesbye, *Distracted Driving*. Farmington Hills, MI: Greenhaven, 2011.

Barron H. Lerner, *One for the Road: Drunk Driving Since 1900*. Baltimore: Johns Hopkins University Press, 2011.

James B. Link, *Driving You Safely: Tips and Advice for Sane, Sensible, and Safe Driving*. Seattle: CreateSpace, 2012.

Valerie Mendralla and Janet Grosshandler, *Drinking and Driving. Now What?* New York: Rosen, 2011.

Internet Sources

Automobile Association of America, "Distracted Driving." http://drivinglaws.aaa.com/laws/distracted-driving.

Distraction.gov, "State Laws." www.distraction.gov/content/get-the-facts/state-laws.html.

Edgar Snyder & Associates, "Cell Phone & Texting Accident Statistics," www.edgarsnyder.com/car-accident/cell-phone/cell-phone-statistics.html.

Governors Highway Safety Association, "Distracted Driving." www.ghsa.org/html/issues/distraction/index.html.

Governors Highway Safety Association, "Graduated Driver Licensing (GDL) Laws." www.ghsa.org/html/stateinfo/laws/licenselaws .html.

Pew Research Center, "Teens and Distracted Driving," November 16, 2009. www.distraction.gov/download/research-pdf /PIP_Teens_and_Distracted_Driving.pdf.

Maria Trimarchi, "Do Car GPS Devices Cause Accidents?," How Stuff Works. http://electronics.howstuffworks.com/gadgets /automotive/car-gps-accidents.htm.

Index

devices in, 71
increase in subscriptions for, 38
percentage of traffic accidents caused by, 29
prevalence of use
among youth, 20–21
while driving, 77
use at accident scenes, 31
Centers for Disease Control and Prevention (CDC), 9
on distracted driving, 8
on driving under the influence, 11, 55, 62, 64
cognitive distractions, 9, 29–30
Consumer Reports (magazine), 9
Coutinho, Albert, 11

deaths. *See* traffic deaths
Department of Health & Human Services, US (DHHS), 57, 63
Department of Transportation, US, 9, 69
Deveau, Aaron, 26–27, 28
Dewing, Jarad, 24
Dickmeyer, Jacob, 70
distracted driving
age group with highest incidence of, 51
drunk driving *vs.,* 33–35
education programs to prevent, 68–69
injuries/deaths from, 8–9
prevalence of, 12, 25
reasons teens engage in, 47

distractions
cognitive, 29–30
teens' perception of drinking/eating as, 41
types of, 9, 29
Dorsey, Kenneth, 8
drivers
bad, 35–37
overconfidence of, 40
driving
eating while, 41–43
nighttime, 14, 25
GDLs and restrictions on, 16–20
driving under the influence
decline in, among teens, 11, 62
distracted driving *vs.,* 33–35
prevalence among teens, 11

Every 15 Minutes Program, 57–59
criticism of, 60–61

Facebooking, 75
Fell, James C., 60–61
Fette, Bernie, 14
Florida, restrictions on teen driving in, 14–16

Geigner, Timothy, 35, 36–37
Governors Highway Safety Association (GHSA), 9, 12
GPS (global positioning system), 20, 71, 77
blocking of, while car is moving, 73

as driving distraction, 43–45
voice-controlled, 77
graduated driving laws
(GDLs), 16
effectiveness of, 18–20
stages of, 17–18

Hardy, Ed, 76
Heiman, Amanda, 70
Hersman, Barbara Deborah,
65–66
Highway Loss Data Institute
(HLDI), 66
Hyman, Ira, 48

Insurance Institute for
Highway Safety, 41

James, Desaleen Rayna, 52, 53,
54
Johnson, Tamara Nicole, 52,
53

Kilmer, Jimm, 56
King, Douglas, 67

LaHood, Ray, 71
Lawson, Davonne, 62–63
LeBeau, Phil, 34–35
Lee, John, 76
Lund, Adrian, 66

Madden, Fred, 11–12
manual distractions, 9
Mariah's Challenge, 56, 64
Massachusetts Institute of
Technology (MIT), 35

McCarthy, Leo, 56
McComber, Robert, 72
McCrindle, Mark, 48
McEwan, Brianna, 8, 10
McNaull, Justin, 49–50
minimum drinking age
debate over lowering, 17
federal, impact on alcohol-
related traffic deaths, 14
Monash University, 25
Mothers Against Drunk
Driving (MADD), 61–62
MP3 players/iPods, 23–24,
74–76
percentage of new vehicles
offering connectivity to, 77
multitasking, 47–48

National Distracted Driving
Awareness Month, 77
National Highway Traffic
Safety Administration
(NHTSA), 10, 64, 69, 77
on eating/drinking while
driving, 41
on impact of federal
minimum drinking age, 14
on percentage of traffic
accidents related to driver
inattention, 9
on prevalence of texting, 51
on texting and risk of traffic
accidents, 30
National Minimum Drinking
Age Act (1985), 14, 17
National Safety Council
(NSC), 25, 29, 30, 38, 47

on multitasking, 47–48

National Transportation Safety Board (NTSB), 50, 65, 70–71

Okrusch, Chad, 56
opinion polls. *See* surveys

Patterson, Angela, 12
Pediatrics (journal), 16
PEMCO, 40
Pew Research Center, 20, 21, 38, 51
Phillips, Jonathon, 28
polls. *See* surveys

Rader, Russ, 72–73
Read, Richard, 48, 71
Reimer, Bryan, 36
Richards, Jenice, 52–53
Rilling, Harry, 8
risk-taking, 45–46
Royal Automobile Club (RAC), 40

SADD (Students Against Destructive Decisions), 64
Sauer, Taylor, 75
Seventeen (magazine)
on distracted driving, 25, 41
on percentage of teens who eat while driving, 43
on percentage of teens who text while driving, 50
on reasons teens engage in distracted driving, 47
Shelley, David Alan, 39

Stegner, Melissa, 61–62
Stimpson, Jim, 21
Strayer, David L., 29–30, 48
Summers, Alexis, 21–22
Sumwalt, Robert, 65
surveys
on involvement in crash/near-crash, by gender and age group, 51
on parents' attitudes toward teen drinking, 64
on reasons teens engage in distracted driving, 47
on teen drinking and driving/binge drinking, 55
on teens' perception of drinking/eating as distractions, 41

Texas Traffic Institute, 14
Texas Transportation Institute (Texas A&M University), 31
texting while driving
effectiveness of bans on, 66
impact on response time, 27–28
length of time drivers take eyes off road during, 38
number of states banning, 77
prevalence of, 51
traffic accidents
caused by texting *vs.* cell phone conversations, 30–32
cell phone-related, 29
as major cause of death, 25
nighttime, 25

Picture Credits

About the Author

Patricia D. Netzley has written over fifty books for children, teens, and adults. She has also worked as an editor and a writing instructor. She is a member of the Society of Children's Book Writers and Illustrators (SCBWI).